HARDPRESS.NET
HOME OF HARD-TO-FIND BOOKS

A Tribute to the Memory of the Pilgrims
by Joel Hawes

Address:
HardPress
8345 NW 66TH ST #2561
MIAMI FL 33166-2626
USA
Email: info@hardpress.net

יהוה

INSTITVTIO THEOLOGICA

ANDOVER FVNDATA MDCCCVII.

ΑΚΡΟΓΩΝΙ... ...ΟΥ ΧΡΙΣΤΟΥ.

Ps. CXIX.
169.
בדברך
הביני

JOH. XVII.
17.
ὁ λογος
ὁ σος
αληθεια
εστι·

A

TRIBUTE

TO THE

MEMORY OF THE PILGRIMS,

AND

A VINDICATION OF THE

CONGREGATIONAL CHURCHES

OF NEW-ENGLAND.

BY JOEL HAWES,

PASTOR OF THE FIRST CHURCH IN HARTFORD.

HARTFORD:

PUBLISHED BY PACKARD & BUTLER.

1830.

G. F. OLMSTED......PRINT......HARTFORD.

TO THE MEMBERS

OF THE

THREE CONGREGATIONAL CHURCHES AND SOCIETIES

IN HARTFORD,

BEFORE WHOM THE FOLLOWING LECTURES WERE DELIVERED,

AND AT WHOSE REQUEST THEY ARE NOW PUBLISHED,

THEY ARE AFFECTIONATELY

INSCRIBED,

BY THE AUTHORS

PREFACE.

The following Lectures were delivered on successive Sabbath evenings during the months of March and April of the present year. It would be trite to say that they were written without any reference to publication, and are committed to the press at the request of friends. Such however is the simple fact. The discussion was commenced for the benefit of the author's own charge, and with no purpose of extending it beyond two or three discourses. It was so announced to the audience. But as the subject was pursued, it increased in interest and presented other and important topics of remark, and was therefore continued much beyond the author's original design.

After he had consented to the publication of the Lectures, it was his intention to give them a careful revision, that he might correct those inaccuracies in style and language which necessarily attend the first draught of a composition. But the pressure of daily employments, together with feeble health, has rendered this impracticable; and he is now compelled to commit the work to the press with only expressing his regret at defects which he is unable to supply. This, however, is not offered as an apology for errors in sentiment, or for mis-statement of material facts. If in these respects, the author has in any case fallen into mistakes, he can only say that it has not been for the want of a desire to know, nor of sincere endeavors to ascertain the truth.

As in delivering the Lectures, the author considered himself to be addressing friends, he used much plainness of speech, and commented with freedom on sentiments held by some, who belong to denominations different from his own. If in this particular, any thing he may have said shall wound christian charity, or furnish just cause of offence to any of the sincere friends of Christ, none would more deeply regret it than himself. That he is strongly opposed to certain pretensions, which are advanced by some, respecting the external order of the church, he is willing to avow; and he is so, because he sincerely believes that such pretensions are contrary to the spirit and doctrine of the scriptures, and of pernicious tendency. But he utterly disclaims every feeling of alienation or uncharitableness towards any who bear the christian name, simply because they are not of the same denomination with himself, or may differ from him in their form of church polity and modes of worship. With perfect truth he can repeat the sentiment, which is more than once advanced in the Lectures—*Grace be with all them who love our Lord Jesus Christ in sincerity.* That the spirit of this Apostolic salutation may more and more extensively pervade the minds and be manifested in the lives of all who profess to be christians, is the author's highest wish and fervent prayer.

Hartford, August, 1830.

Note. To prevent mistake the author thinks it proper to state, that his remarks in the first Lecture, respecting the constitution and order of the primitive churches, are not confined to the age of the Apostles, but generally to the first two centuries after Christ.

CONTENTS.

LECTURE I.

Page

Constitution and Order of the Primitive Churches, 1

LECTURE II.

Origin, Principles, and Influence of the Congregational Churches of New-England, - - - 41

LECTURE III.

Deductions from the foregoing Lectures, - - 79

LECTURE IV.

Character and Vindication of the Pilgrims, - - 109

LECTURE V.

Causes and Extent of Declension in the Congregational Churches of New-England. - - - 145

LECTURE VI.

Means of Recovery and Defence, - - - - - 185

LECTURE I.

CONSTITUTION AND ORDER OF THE PRIMITIVE CHURCHES.

JEREMIAH, vi. 16.

THUS SAITH THE LORD, STAND IN THE WAYS AND SEE, AND ASK FOR THE OLD PATHS, WHERE IS THE GOOD WAY, AND WALK THEREIN, AND YE SHALL FIND REST FOR YOUR SOULS.

I PROPOSE in this, and some additional lectures, to present an outline of the constitution and order of the primitive churches, with special reference to an illustration of the principles and polity of the Congregational churches of New England. It is with no purpose to excite controversy, that I call your attention to this subject. In the discussion of it, I shall, doubtless, be led to advance sentiments, not altogether in accordance with those that are held by some other denominations of christians. This is the exercise of a common right. We all claim the privilege of explaining and defending our own views of truth and duty; and if this is done in the spirit of candor and kindness, no one has any cause of complaint. I am not accustomed, as you know, to at-

1

tach much importance to mere forms and ceremonies, much less, to attack the forms and ceremonies of other denominations. These are matters, which I regard as comparatively of small moment ; and in judging of the expediency of adopting them in religious worship, I readily concede to others the same liberty that I claim for myself. I fully believe, with the Apostle, that in Christ Jesus, neither circumcision availeth any thing, nor uncircumcision, but a new creature ; and that while one saith I am of Paul, and another, I am of Apollos, and another, I am of Cephas, unless we are all of Christ, imbued with his spirit and devoted to his service, we cannot see the kingdom of God. "Every believer in Jesus," says an eminent Episcopalian, "who is a partaker of the grace of God in truth, is a member of the true church, to whatever particular denomination of christians he may belong ; without this, Popes, Bishops, Presbyters, Pastors or Deacons, are but the limbs of Antichrist, and of the synagogue of Satan, and belong to no church which the great Shepherd and Bishop of souls will acknowledge for his own."* Let it not be supposed however, that because I do not consider the outward form or polity of the church, as of the essentials of religion, I therefore regard it as a mat-

* Miller's Letters, p. 24.

ter of entire indifference. This would be a great mistake. The garment you wear is no part of your person, " either of your soul or your body," and yet one garment may be more convenient than another; or it may be so inconvenient as to be scarcely capable of being worn. In like manner, though forms of church government and modes of worship are no essential part of religion, yet one form of government and mode of worship may be better adapted to promote the cause of religion than another ; and they may be so corrupted and changed from the simplicity of the original institution, as directly to counteract and defeat the great end of religion.*

The subject, then, proposed for consideration is one of importance ; and I cannot but hope, that a discussion of it may lead you to *stand in the way and see, and to ask for the old paths, where is the good way, and to walk therein, that you may find rest for your souls.*

There are, moreover, at the present time, some special reasons for calling your attention to this subject. As a general fact, it is a subject, I apprehend, but little understood by the members of our churches. It is rarely discussed, either from the pulpit or the press ; and while we are all sensible,

* Campbell's Lectures on Eccles. Hist. p. 128.

that great and precious blessings have flowed to us, from the religious institutions of our fathers, there are but few among us, I fear, who clearly understand the *principles* of those institutions, or are properly qualified to defend them, when attacked. And attacked they often are, at the present day, and that, with no small share of acrimony and violence. Misrepresentations are made, and claims advanced, which strike at the very foundation of the ancient churches of New England; and though in years past, the number and moral power of these churches may have sufficed to render such misrepresentations and assaults comparatively harmless, the times have changed, and it has become important to adopt other means of defence. We must, as a denomination, understand the nature and tendency of that form of church polity which has come down to us from our fathers. The principles of Congregationalism must be explained; their accordance with the scriptures and with primitive practice demonstrated; their adaptation to the genius of our civil institutions pointed out, and their happy influence in promoting vital godliness and all the best interests of men illustrated and enforced.

To accomplish some of these objects, in respect to the people of my own charge, is the end I propose in attempting this service. May the Spirit of all grace guide me in the prosecution of it, and crown the effort with an abundant blessing.

The first question I propose to consider is, whether Christ, or his Apostles established any particular form of ecclesiastical polity, as of universal obligation? In other words, do the scriptures furnish us with any precise instruction, respecting the external form of the church, or the method according to which it should be governed? The affirmative of this question, as you are aware, is asserted by some with an air of confidence, that would seem to preclude the possibility of a doubt respecting it. We are told by the advocates of what are very properly called *high church notions*, "that one form of government for the church is unalterably fixed by divine appointment; that this form is Episcopal; that it is absolutely essential to the existence of the church; that, of course, wherever it is wanting, there is no church, no regular ministry, no valid ordinances; and that all who are united to religious societies, not conformed to this order, are "aliens from Christ," "out of the appointed road to heaven," and have no hope but in the uncovenanted mercies of God."

These exclusive claims, I am aware, are rejected by a great number of the most intelligent and pious

1*

Episcopalians in our country and in England ; but they are also asserted, in all their offensiveness, by a still greater, and I fear, growing number, in that denomination.

Now before any one should presume to advance such claims, he ought, certainly, to be able to adduce the *fullest* and most *decided* authority in support of them. But where is such authority to be found ? Is it furnished in the gospel of Jesus Christ, or in the writings of his Apostles ? To me nothing seems plainer, than that it is not. I have read the Christian scriptures in vain, if in any one chapter or verse the subject of church government is formally discussed, or any thing like a system of polity laid down as of universal obligation. That our Lord Jesus Christ established a church and appointed certain officers in it, is admitted by all. But that he prescribed the exact form of the church, or the order of its government, or the mode of ordaining its ministers, is no where taught in the New Testament, and is, I am persuaded, a sentiment having no other foundation, than the authority of men.

Accordingly a multitude of Episcopalians, both Bishops and others, readily acknowledge that the scriptures no where establish any particular form of church government. This is well known to have been the opinion of *all* the English reformers; and in later times, it has been held by such men as Locke, and Bacon, and Stillingfleet, and Tillotson, and Leighton, and Reynolds, and Burnet, and Croft, and a long list of others, the brightest lights that have ever shone in the English church. To these witnesses, I will add two others of more modern date. Archdeacon Payley says; "It cannot be proved, that any form of church government was laid down in the Christian scriptures, with a view of fixing a constitution for succeeding ages." The Editors of the Christian Observer in their number for March, 1804 say, "that Episcopalians found not the merits of their cause, upon any express injunction or delineation of church government in the scriptures, for there is none."

On the fact here conceded, I have three remarks to make. 1. From the silence of Christ and his Apostles on the subject, it is entirely certain, that *they* regarded no particular form of ecclesiastical polity as essential, either to the existence of the church, the authority of its ministry, or the validity of its ordinances. If the outward form of the church, or the mode of constituting its ministry is a matter of such importance, that there can be no church, and no ministry unless they are organized and appointed in a particular way, it is incredible, that our divine Lord and his inspired messengers should have passed by the subject, in so much silence, and no where have delivered any explicit instructions respecting it. The truth is, our Lord Jesus Christ, by leaving this matter undetermined, has left his churches a discretionary power of modelling their form of government, according to their views of expediency and the general principles of the gospel. Had he intended to establish any uniform mode of government, he would have legislated explicitly on the subject, and laid down specific rules, according to which the church should be governed in all future ages. But he has not done this; and therefore every church has a right to make laws for itself, provided that these laws are consistent with charity and with the fundamental doctrines of christianity.*

2. It is an unauthorized assumption of power, and a grievous offence against charity, to make any particular form of church government or mode of worship a condition of christian fellowship and communion. Whatever the scriptures have decided on this subject is of divine authority; but nothing else is of such authority, or at all binding on the consciences of men. But the scriptures have no where decided

* Mosheim, vol. 1 : 85.

that any particular form of government, or mode of ordination is essential to the existence of the church, or the authority of its ministry, or the validity of its ordinances.   Those, then, who affirm, that there can be no true church, or ministry, or ordinances, but such as are constituted and administered in a particular way, assume to themselves the right of deciding in matters which the great Head of the church has left undecided ; and when they proceed to make a compliance with *their prescribed* rites and ceremonies, a condition of fellowship with other christians and churches, they sin against charity, and violate the great principles of peace and unity in the church of God.   Without any authority from Christ, or his Apostles, and contrary to the whole spirit and tenor of the gospel, they place a point of external order, on a par with the essence of religion ; and in so doing, virtually excommunicate from the church of God, a very great proportion of the protestant world—declaring them to be 'out of the appointed way to heaven,' and having no hope, but in the ' uncovenanted mercy of God.'   Can this be right?   Is there any thing in the spirit or precepts of the gospel to justify principles like these ?

That such high and exclusive claims should be advanced by Roman Catholics, claiming infallibility, is what might be expected ; but that they should be advanced by Protestants, professing to take the Bible for their guide, is more than one could believe, if the fact were not attested by the most indubitable evidence. To me nothing seems plainer than the principle laid down by Robert Hall, in his Treatise on Communion,* that 'no man or body of men has a right to make that a condition of communion, which is not in the New Testament made a condition of salvation.' This principle approves itself to the common sense and conscience of every man, and runs through the whole tenor of the christian scriptures. It ought to be adopted as a fundamental principle in all the churches of our Lord Jesus Christ ; and every departure from it, every attempt to erect forms and ceremonies into terms of christian communion, ought to be regarded as a violation of the very spirit of the gospel, and as the worst sort of heresy.†

* p. 4. Preface.

† The term is here used according to its meaning in the original, as denoting sect or party, and needs no qualification.

" Nothing, says Robert Hall, more abhorrent from the principles and maxims of the sacred oracles can be conceived, than the idea of a plurality of true churches, neither in actual communion with each other, nor in a capacity for such communion. Though this rending of the seamless garment of our Saviour, this schism in the members of his mystical body, is by far the greatest calamity which has befallen the christian interest, and

3. I venture another remark. Our Saviour has commanded nothing, expressly, respecting the external form of the church, or the mode of its government. As a natural consequence, christians have formed themselves into different denominations, and have adopted different forms of government, and modes of worship. Is this, *on the whole*, to be regretted? That many and serious evils are occasioned by the existence of different denominations cannot be doubted. But would they have been

one of the most fatal effects of the great apostacy foretold by the sacred penman, we have been so long familiarized to it as to be scarcely sensible of its enormity, nor does it excite surprise or concern, in any degree proportioned to what would be felt by one who had contemplated the church in the first ages. To see christian societies regarding each other with the jealousies of rival empires, each aiming to raise itself on the ruin of all others, making extravagant boasts of superior purity, generally in exact proportion to their departure from it, and scarcely deigning to acknowledge the possibility of obtaining salvation out of their pale, is the odious and disgusting spectacle which modern Christianity presents.

The bond of charity which unites the genuine followers of Christ in distinction from the world, is dissolved, and the very terms by which it was wont to be denoted, exclusively employed to express a predilection for a sect. The evils which result from this state of division are incalculable ; it supplies infidels with their most plausible topics of invective ; it hardens the consciences of the impenitent, weakens the hands of the good, impedes the efficacy of prayer, and is probably the principal obstruction to that ample effusion of the spirit, which is essential to the renovation of the world." *Terms of Communion. p.* 11.

less, had there been but one denomination? Suppose that Christ had prescribed a particular form of government for the church, and had laid down, in minute and circumstantial detail, a ritual of worship and discipline. There would then have been but one denomination of christians in the world. All would have had the same name, the same polity, the same mode of worship. Are we sure that this would have been a blessing? Would there have existed in the church more piety, more zeal, or more efficient activity in promoting the cause of Christ, and the salvation of sinners? We have not the means of deciding this question; but to me, it seems highly probable, that in such a case, the whole church would have been a dead sea; such as it was during the dark ages, when there was, in fact, but one denomination. Deep night brooded over the whole world; and the power of godliness had well nigh become extinct.

Considering how *imperfect men are, even the best of men*, it can hardly admit of doubt, that it is better for the church and the world, that different denominations should exist. And this was probably one reason why Christ did not establish any one invariable form of government for his church. Nor is there any thing in what is here said, that implies indifference to essential error, or fellowship with de-

.nominations that deny the fundamental doctrines of the gospel. Such denominations there are; and the Bible forbids us to have any fellowship with them, lest we be partakers of their evil deeds.*

But there is nothing in the Bible, or in the nature of the case, which need prevent *real christians,* to whatever denomination they belong, from uniting, on the ground of their common christianity, and treating each other as members of the same body, and of the household of faith. Episcopalians, Baptists, Methodists, Presbyterians, Congregationalists and others, while they hold the fundamentals of the gospel, might retain their distinctive principles, and yet be on terms of the most cordial fellowship and communion. This, indeed, is what constitutes the true unity of the church. It is a unity, not in forms and ceremonies; nor in points of unessential doctrine and practice; but in kindness and love, and a harmonious assent to the fundamental truths of the gospel. This is the only unity that is worth striving for; and all who break this unity by setting up outward forms as terms of communion ought to be regarded, as they were in primitive times, as "schismatics" and "violators of the church's unity and concord."†

* 2 John, 11   † King on the Primitive Church, p. 154—169.

Let us now pass to consider the constitution and order of the primitive churches.

I. *The constitution of these churches.*

Under the preaching of Christ and his Apostles, great multitudes were converted to christianity. These were collected into distinct societies, larger or smaller, as the case might be, each of which was accustomed to meet in the same place for the purpose of social worship and the enjoyment of christian ordinances.   Such was the church of Philippi, the church of Ephesus, the church of Antioch, the church of Rome.   They were distinct, independent congregations of christians, assembling together for religious exercises.   The organization of these churches, was extremely simple.   They were voluntary associations of holy men and women meeting together on terms of perfect equality, for purposes purely religious ; united in faith and love, and cementing their union, as they had opportunity, by a joint participation in religious offices ; in adoration and praise, and in commemorating the sufferings of their common Lord and Savior.   They had no sacrifices, nor images, nor oracles, nor sacerdotal orders, nor splendid ritual, nor any thing of that pomp and show which were subsequently introduced to corrupt and debase the simplicity of christian worship.

Acting on the principle laid down by our Savior, that his kingdom is not of this world, the primitive churches stood out from all connexion with civil government, and never in the least interfered in the affairs of the state. Each church was independent of every other, forming by itself a little republic, governed by its own laws and regulating, by a common vote of the brethren, all its internal concerns.* There is no evidence, that the churches were joined together by association, confederation or any bonds, but those of charity and a mutual interchange of kind offices, till the middle of the second century. The power of enacting laws, of appointing teachers and ministers, of determining controversies, of administering descipline, of expelling and of receiving again into communion unworthy members, was lodged in

---

* " Although all the churches were, in the first age of Christianity, united together in one common bond of faith and love, and were in every respect ready to promote the interests and welfare of each other, by a reciprocal interchange of good offices ; yet with regard to government and internal economy, every individual church considered itself as an independent community, none of them ever looking in these respects, beyond the circle of its own members for assistance, or recognizing any sort of external influence or authority." *Moshiem's Commentaries. vol.* 1, *p.* 263–5.

Every one must perceive that the fact here stated by the learned Moshiem is totally irreconcilable with the notion that government by Diocesan bishops existed in the primitive churches.

each particular church, nor could the pastors either resolve or sanction any thing whatever without the knowledge and concurrence of the general body of christians, of which the church was composed.*

* Since the delivery of these Lectures, the author has been favored with the perusal of three very interesting manuscript Lectures by Dr. Murdock, on the same general subject. From the eighth Lecture in the series, he is permitted to make the following extract.

"The supreme power was in the assembled fraternity, or in the whole body of christians composing the association, or church. Respect was paid of course, and necessarily, to the inspired Apostles, and to the men of most talents and weight of character. Yet even the Apostles did not claim dominion, or jurisdiction over these associations, as being their constituted Lords and Governors. As inspire men, as the Apostles of Jesus Christ, and the persons who, under God, had converted many of the associated individuals,—they spoke in a higher and more decisive tone than ordinary brethren ; and were heard with far greater reverence and respect. Yet they did not take upon them to decide the questions which came before a church, as if they alone had authority. They stated their views, offered reasons for their opinions, and then invited the brethren to decide the case. The procedure at the election of Mathias† to succeed Judas, in the creation and appointment of the seven Deacons, and in determining the question respecting the duty of Gentile converts to obey the laws of Moses, affords us both proof and illustration of this point.

And so in all Paul's Epistles, he speaks with assurance, as being an inspired man, and he commands and exhorts ; yet without taking the decision of any ecclesiastical question out of the hands of the church or associated brotherhood. Even in the clear and strong case of the incestuous person at Corinth, he did not assume

† Acts ii.   Acts vii.   Acts xv.   Mosheim's Com. p. 210.

Such is a general view of the order of the primitive churches, as it may be gathered from the records of the New Testament and the writings of the earliest christian fathers.

2. Let us next consider what officers were appointed in these churches. The Apostles were extraordinary ministers. They received their commission directly from the Lord Jesus Christ. They had no stated charge. Their field was the world. In their apostolic character, they had no successors. Their office expired with themselves. Besides these, there were other extraordinary ministers, such as prophets and evangelists and some others.* Their office, it would seem, was temporary, adapted to the peculiar exigences of the church in that day, and terminated when the circumstances which gave rise to

the power of excommunicating the offender, but only called upon the brethren to do this duty, by meeting together, and casting out the man forthwith.† Neither can an example be adduced from all the New Testament, of the Apostles, individually or collectively, appointing any man to office, in any church, without the previous consent and election of that church; or of their deciding, *judicially*, any case of discipline, or any proper ecclesiastical question, by their own power and authority. So careful were these faithful ambassadors of Christ, not to lord it over God's heritage, and not to infringe upon the power of every church to manage its own affairs, itself paying due regard to the best light afforded to it."

* Eph. iv. 11.   † 1 Cor. v. 3—7.

2*

it ceased to exist. Setting aside these, there were only two classes of permanent officers in the primitive church; bishops, or as they are commonly called, presbyters and deacons. During the lives of the Apostles, and for a considerable time after, there was generally a plurality* of presbyters or bishops in each church, who presided over its government and instruction with equal and co-ordinate authority. No one claimed any precedence or superiority over others, nor exercised any, but what was voluntarily conceded to him on account of his superior wisdom, piety, and weight of character. These presbyters or bishops were chosen by the people, and were consecrated by their fellow presbyters to their office, by prayer and the imposition of hands.† As they were chosen by the free suffrages of the people, so they were supported by their voluntary oblations. They presided in their assemblies, conducted their worship, and assisted in maintaining government and discipline ; but as just remarked, they had no power to enact laws or establish rules for the regulation of the church without the consent and concurrence of its members.

As for bishops, considered as an order of ministers, distinct from presbyters, there is no evidence of the

* Acts xx. 17.   Philip i. 1.   Moshiem's Com. vol. 1. p. 219.
† 1 Tim. iv. 14.

existence of any such order in the primitive church. Most certainly its existence and authority are no where recognized in the New Testament. It probably soon became customary for the presbyters in a particular church to appoint one of their number as a sort of moderator or president, *a primus inter pares.* But this gave him no additional authority as a minister, nor any right to extend his jurisdiction a step beyond the limits of his own church or parish. After the most careful examination which I have been able to give to the subject, I am prepared to say, that nothing like a modern diocesan bishop, *claiming the exclusive right of ordination, confirmation and government, and presiding over the churches of an extended province,* existed in the church till near the close of the second century.

This is not the place to exhibit, in detail, the evidence of this position. Some of the *topics* of argument are the following.

The first ministers of Christ were all considered as equals ; they were required to be so by their divine Lord, and not to assume or exercise any authority over one another.* They all received and acted under one and the same commission ; and could not, therefore, be invested with different, but with the

* Mark x. 42—45 : Luke xxii. 25.

same authority.* They were called by the same names, bishops and elders being terms of the same import, and convertible, one for the other, as used in the New Testament.† As they were designated by the same names and invested with the same authority, so they were required to possess the same qualifications and were appointed to perform the same duties. They all had an equal right to preach, to baptize, to ordain‡ to rule§ in the church, and to perform all the functions of the sacred office.‖

In some of the churches, as at Ephesus and Phillippi,¶ there were a number of bishops, who governed in their respective churches as co-ordinate rulers or as a common council. In no part of the New Testament, do we find the least notice taken of any church or number of churches, having been subject to the authority of a single man. In none of the addresses or salutations to the churches, contained in the Acts of the Apostles and in the Epistles, are bishops once mentioned as an order of ministers *distinct* from presbyters, or in any respect superior to them. Both bishops and presbyters received the same

---

* Math. xxviii. 19, 20.

† Acts xx. 17, compared with verse 28 : Titus i. 5, 7 : 1 Peter v. 1, 2 : also, see King on the primitive church, p. 67.

‡ 1 Tim. iv. 14 : Acts xiv. 23.

§ 1 Tim. iii. 2, 4, 5 ; v. 17 ; i. 22.   ‖ Miller's Letters, p. 41.

¶ Acts xx 17—28 : Phil. i. 1, 2.

ordination, and no instance occurs either in the New Testament or in the history of the two first centuries, in which a bishop was otherwise ordained than a presbyter.

The Bible, then, furnishes no authority in support of the order of bishops as a distinct class of ministers. Its authority is decidedly against such an order. No matter then how early this order existed. If it is not authorized by the scriptures, it is of human origin ; and has no right to claim supremacy as if it were of divine appointment.*

* It is often asked with an air of triumph, as if the question admitted of no answer, *how* and *when* episcopacy was introduced into the church, if it was not of apostolic origin. Those who think there is any difficulty in answering this question, would do well to consult Miller's Letters and Dr. Campbell's Lectures on Ecclesiastical History. The rise of episcopacy in the church can very easily be traced, and is well sketched in the following language of Dr. Chauncy. " The bishop was no more than *primus inter pares*, the head presbyter, the præses or moderator of the consistory, and it was by gradual steps he attained to the power with which he was afterwards vested. These ecclesiastical superiorities and inferiorities, which have for a long time been visible in the Christian world, were unknown in the first and purest ages : nor did they at once take place. It was the work of time. From prime-presbyters, arose city-bishops ; from city-bishops, diocesan ones ; from diocesan bishops, metropolitans ; from metropolitans, patriarchs ; and finally, at the top of all, *his holiness the pope*, claiming the character of universal head of the church." *Dud. Lect. p.* 84.

Chauncy's view of Episcopacy. Miller's Letters. Dwight's System. Mosheim's Hist. and Comm.

But what is the testimony of antiquity on this subject? The early fathers, such as Clemens Romanus, Ignatius, Polycarp, Tertullian, Justin Martyr and others, who lived within the second century, though they often mention the officers of the church, take no notice of more than two orders, bishops and deacons, nor once intimate that any distinction existed between bishops and elders, but with one voice declare them to be of the same order.* Added to this, it was the opinion of the first reformers in the church of England, that there is, according to the gospel, no distinction between bishops and presbyters. " In a celebrated work called The Institution of a Christian Man, approved expressly by Archbishop Cranmer, Bishops Jewell, Willet and Stillingfleet, and the main body of the English clergy, together with the King and Parliament, is this declaration." " In the New Testament there is no mention of any other degrees, but of deacons or ministers, and of presbyters or bishops."† Dr. Reynolds, professor of divinity in

---

* After the author had consented to the publication of these Lectures, it was his intention to present, in the form of notes, a brief argument in support of each of the above positions with quotations from the Fathers. But he soon found that this would require a volume, instead of a few short notes. He was therefore obliged to relinquish his purpose, and only to refer to his principal authorities in the margin.

† Dwight's Sys. vol. 5, p. 191.

Oxford, declares that all who had labored for five hundred years before his time, taught that all pastors whether entitled bishops or priests, have equal power and authority by God's word ; and this, he adds, is the common judgment of the reformed churches of Switzerlànd, Savoy, France, Germany, Hungary, Poland, the Netherlands, Scotland and England." Nor is there any evidence, that, among Protestants the perfect equality of bishops and presbyters was ever publicly denied, or the exclusive divine right of Episcopacy ever asserted, till 1588.　In January of that year, Dr. Bancroft,* chaplain of Archbishop Whitgift, undertook to prove in a sermon, that the ' bishops of England were a distinct order from priests, and had superiority over them *jure divino*, and directly from God.'　' This, says the historian Neal, was *new* and *strange* doctrine to the churchmen of these times.'　But it has now become an old and common doctrine, and its advocates, it grieves me to say it, are increasing in number, and in the exclusiveness of their pretensions——pretensions which deny to all ministers, but such as have been ordained by a bishop, the right to preach the gospel, and administer the sacraments; and which pronounce the churches of all other denominations, except the episcopal, to be

* Neal, vol. 1, 558.

irregular and unscriptural. And all this in the 19th century! Truly, when one hears this, he can hardly refrain from thinking, that since the time of Edward the sixth, the reformation, in respect to some people at least, has been rather retrograde, than progressive. *Then,* Calvin, and Knox, and Bucer, and Fagius and Tremellius and Peter Martyr, though foreigners and Presbyterians, were openly acknowledged by the English reformers, as true ministers of Christ. The last four of these illustrious men, without any question as to the validity of their ordination, were employed as professors of Divinity in the Universities of Oxford and Cambridge; and Knox, it is well known, when compelled to flee from Scotland, was received with open arms, by the fathers of the church of England, and without reordination was allowed to preach in all their pulpits. He was also appointed one of the chaplains to Edward the sixth; and when the book of common prayer was undergoing a revisal, he assisted in that work. He was likewise employed in revising the articles of religion previous to their ratification by Parliament.* All this, it would seem, was irregular; and we are now told that none have a right to preach, or administer

* M'Crie's Life of Knox. Period III.

the sacraments but those who have received ordination from a bishop. With Episcopalians, who disclaim, and many do disclaim these high pretensions, I have no controversy. Holding, as many of them do, the essentials of the gospel ; and truly devoted, as many of them are, to the cause of our common Master, *I bid them God speed with all my heart.* I complain only of those who assert that their's is the only true, Apostolic church, and their's the only authorized ministry, and their's the only valid ordinances, and who, by their assumptions on this subject, declare all other churches schismatical, and all other ministers mere intruders into the sacred office, and their ministrations null and void. Before I can admit such claims, I must examine them; and if I find them unauthorized, and unscriptural, I hold myself bound to resist them, as opposed to the whole spirit of the gospel, and a gross violation of the great law of christian love and concord.

But I gladly quit this topic. I have touched upon it from no love of controversy, nor from any wish to wound the feelings, or disturb the peace of any individual who may choose to worship God in a different communion from that to which I belong. But as it is a topic on which much is said and written at the present day, and which is frequently obtruded

3

upon our attention, I felt it my duty to say thus much upon it, to convince you, my friends, if indeed any of you need to be convinced, that the argument is, to say the least, not *all* on one side.

3. Let us next consider the manner in which persons were received into the primitive church. Our Lord Jesus Christ came into the world to set up a spiritual kingdom, and he required that all, who became members of his church, should be holy persons. On this principle the primitive churches were formed. The Apostles and first teachers of christianity required of all, whom they received to the special ordinances of the gospel, an open profession of their faith in Christ, and a solemn engagement to live in obedience to his commands. Hence Origen says : "We do our utmost, that our assemblies be composed of good and wise men, so that none who are admitted to our congregations, and prayers, are vicious and wicked, except very rarely it may happen, that a particular bad man may be concealed in so great a number." In the earliest times of the church, it was customary to receive persons to baptism and the communion *immediately* on their profession of faith and hopeful conversion. Such was the fact in regard to the three thousand who were converted on the day of Pentecost ; and also in the case

of Cornelius, of Lydia, and the Jailor. This custom, however, was soon discontinued, probably, during the life time of the Apostles, and then none were admitted to baptism but such as had been previously instructed ; and by a season of trial, had given satisfactory evidence of pious dispositions and sincere intentions. Hence arose the order of catechumens,—a class of persons who were candidates for membership in the church, and who were carefully instructed, with reference to their being admitted to the special ordinance of the gospel.* How long they were continued in this state of preparation does not appear. Probably the season of probation varied with circumstances ;—was sometimes longer and sometimes shorter, according to the age and character of the candidates. The object was two fold— that they might be instructed in the principles of the gospel, and evince by a change in their lives and habits, the sincerity of their professed conversion. It was a wise and most salutary regulation, and ought to be adopted in all the churches of Christ. Nothing can tend more directly to corrupt the church and destroy its moral power, than the practice of admitting persons to communion before they have had time to

* See Mosheim vol, 1. p. 99, also Cave's Primitive Christianity, p. 305.

test the reality of their religion, or to show by their
lives, whether they are worthy subjects to be enroll-
ed among the disciples of Christ.*

As the primitive churches were exceedingly cautious in receiving persons into their communion, so
they were strict to maintain discipline, and to exclude
from their society all unworthy and depraved members. 'The holy or good christians of those times,'
says an old writer, 'were infinitely careful to keep the
honor of their religion unspotted, to stifle every sin in
its birth, and by bringing offenders to public shame
and penalty, to keep them from propagating the malignant influence of a bad example.' For this purpose,
they watched over one another, told them privately of
their faults, brought them before the cognizance of
the church ; and as the case might be, suspended or
cut off from communion those who walked disorderly and could not be reclaimed by milder methods.
It is needless to specify particular offences, since
none were spared. They aimed to keep the
churches in the faith and purity of the gospel, and by
investing them with a holy, spotless character, to
have them answer the great end of their institution ;

* See a valuable discussion of this subject in the Christian
Spectator, for June, 1830, p. 254.

the maintenance and dissemination of light and holiness in the world.'*

That infant baptism was practiced in the primitive churches admits of no reasonable doubt. To say nothing of the scriptural authority for this practice, the earliest historical records† furnish the fullest evidence that christian parents were in the habit of dedicating their children to God in the ordinance of baptism. To adults this ordinance was never administered but on a profession of faith, and then usually by immersion, though not always. The quantity of water used, or the manner of applying it, was not deemed essential, nor ought it to be so considered at the present day. The thing signified in baptism is the only thing worth contending for ; and since we and our Baptist brethren are perfectly agreed on this point, it is deeply to be lamented, that any among them are disposed to make the *mere mode of ceremony, the cut of a coat,* a condition of communion, or a wall of separation between them and other christians. So did not the primitive christians. They could differ about rites and ceremonies and forms, and yet freely commune with each other and unite in all the varied expressions of

* Cave's Prim. Ch. p. 356.   † See Cave p. 303–308.

3*

christian love and fellowship. And I trust in God, that the day is not far distant, when all christians shall possess the same spirit, and act on the same principle ; when they shall cease to institute terms of communion not authorized in the Bible ; and shall regard and treat each other as children of the same Father and members of the same houschold of faith, though they have *different names and wear different garments.*

4. In regard to the manner of conducting public worship in the primitive churches, it seems to have been something like the following. After the people were assembled, the first service performed was the offering of a short prayer, which seems to have been designed as an invocation of the divine presence and blessing. That this was the uniform practice, is not certain ; but that it was common, Mosheim and Cave think there can be no doubt. After thus opening the service, the scriptures were read, usually by a person appointed for that purpose, who was preparing for the sacred office. The portion read was longer or shorter, according to circumstances, sometimes consisting of a chapter, and sometimes of several chapters. Then the assembly united in singing a psalm or hymn, which was either selected out of the scriptures, particularly from the book of

Psalms, or was of their own composing. In this duty the whole congregation bore a part ; all joining together in celebrating the praises of their God and Saviour. Then followed the preaching of the word. The portion of scripture which had been read, furnished the subject ; and the object of the preacher was to illustrate and enforce what the people had heard from the word of God. His discourse had very little resemblance to a modern sermon. It was a free, glowing, extemporaneous illustration of the divine oracles, and closed with a direct and fervid exhortation to the hearers to believe and practice the sacred lessons which they had heard. When the sermon was ended, which was usually an hour long. the whole congregation rose up to present their common and united prayer to Almighty God. In their public devotions, especially on the sabbath, their posture was always standing. As they accounted that a joyful and glorious day, they deemed it improper to kneel, though they often used this posture in prayer on other occasions. The congregation, standing up, turned their faces towards the east, probably out of respect to Christ, as the sun of the moral world, or from a common opinion that that was the most excellent part of the world ;* and

* See Cave, ch. ix. 288, and King, ch. ii. 27.

then spreading forth their hands, and lifting their
eyes, which were closed, towards heaven, they si-
ently joined in the prayer which was offered by the
president or minister. They did not vocally join in
the prayers, or utter responses ; but simply testified
their assent, at the close, by saying *amen*, or *so let it
be*. Says Tertullian, a father of the second century,
" We do not pray with a monitor, reading our prayers out of a book. No, but on the contrary we pray
de pectore, from the heart, our own heart and soul
dictating to us what is most proper and suitable to
be asked, having no need of any other monitor besides." Justin Martyr, who lived half a century
earlier, says, that the bishop sent up prayers and
praises, *ose dunamis*, according to his ability,—an
expression entirely inconsistent with the supposition
that he used a form of prayer or prayed from a book.
Chancellor King, himself an episcopalian, and one
who examined this subject with great ability, affirms, " That the words or expressions of the prayers
offered in the primitive churches, were not imposed
or prescribed, but every one that officiated delivered
himself in such terms as best pleased him ; and
varied his petitions according to the present circumstances and emergencies ; or if it be more intelligible, he adds, the primitive christians had no stinted

liturgies or imposed forms of prayer."[*] Indeed, liturgies were unknown in the church till towards the close of the 4th centary; nor then was there any one uniform ritual or service prescribed. It was left to every bishop to draw up a form of prayer for his own church [†] After the prayer, the assembly presented their oblations or gifts, which each one, according to his ability, had brought with him. From these offerings the elder or officiating minister took so much as he thought necessary for the celebration of the Lord's Supper, which he consecrated by prayer; the people saying, amen, at the close. This ordinance was usually celebrated at the close of worship every Lord's day, and perhaps in the earliest times of the church, still more frequently, making a part of social worship whenever they engaged in it. After partaking of the Lord's Supper, it was a custom, in many of the churches, for the members to sit down to a sober and sacred repast, called the feast of love. At the breaking up of the assembly, the brethren and sisters exchanged with each other, what from its being a token of mutual good will, was called the kiss of peace. Well may we exclaim with

* King's Prim. Church Part 2. p. 33. To this very able and candid writer, the author is indebted for most of the facts above stated.

† Neal vol. 1, p. 97. Krazer de Liturgiis, sec. 1, chap 1. p. 7.

Mosheim, 'How truly admirable the simplicity by which the rites of our holy religion were characterized in these its infant days.'*

I will detain you but a moment longer, just to notice the manner in which the primitive christians regarded the Sabbath.   There is the fullest evidence that in the time of the Apostles, and indeed from the time of our Savior's resurrection, the first day of the week was kept as a day of holy rest, sacredly devoted to the public and private duties of religion.   On this day the disciples were met, when Christ first appeared to them after he had risen from the dead, and again the next week, or seven days after.   On this day they were assembled, when, at the season of Pentecost, the Holy Ghost descended upon them in his miraculous gifts, and achieved for them the first fruits of the cross, in the conversion of three thousand, under a single sermon.   And frequently, in the Acts of the Apostles, and in the Epistles allusion is made to this day, as a season expressly set apart for the holding of solemn assemblies, and universally regarded by christians as holy time.   In what manner the early christians were accustomed to keep the Sabbath is sufficiently indicated by a passage in Clemens Alexandrinus.   " A true christian, he says,

* Mosheim's Com. vol. 1, p. 262.

according to the commands of Christ, observes the Lord's day, by casting out all evil thoughts, and entertaining all good ones, glorifying the resurrection of the Lord." Justin Martyr also writes : " On the day that is called Sunday, all, both of the country and city, assemble together, where we preach and pray, and discharge all the other usual parts of divine worship." And Dionysius declares : " To-day being the Lord's day, we keep it holy."

The Sabbath was exceedingly precious to the primitive christians. They called it ' the chief of days ;' ' their rest indeed.' They kept it with sacred gladness, as Tertullian affirms, giving themselves to holy joy, and banishing every thing that had the least tendency to, or the least appearance of sorrow and grief, insomuch that they considered it highly improper and wrong either to fast or kneel on that day in their worship.

In regard to fasts and festivals, none were enjoined by Christ or his Apostles ; and none were regarded by the first christians as of divine appointment, though several were introduced at an early date, and were generally observed. The fast of Lent was very ancient, though far enough from having apostolical authority. So the festival of Easter, in commemoration of the resurrection of Christ, was early observed in the churches; and likewise of Whitsunday, or Pentecost, in commemoration of the descent of the Holy Ghost on the Apostles. But no mention is made of Christmas till more than three hundred years after our Saviour's advent, nor is there any evidence that this festival was observed in the church at an earlier period.

As for confirmation, it seems hardly necessary to remark, that it is a rite wholly unauthorized in the scriptures, and not once mentioned in any historical record till two hundred years after Christ. But by that time, it is well known, that a great variety of absurd and unscriptural rites had crept into the church,—such as the use of sponsors in baptism, annointing the body, signing with the sign of the cross, exorcism, and a formal consecration of the water in baptism. All these rites were practiced in the time of Tertullian, who is the first author that takes any notice of confirmation; and if his testimony proves this rite to be of Apostolic origin, it proves the rites above specified to have the same origin.*

* See King on the Prim. Church, Part II. p. 80.

The author is aware that there are three texts, which are usually urged in support of the rite of confirmation. Acts 8 : 14—17. 19 : 6. and Heb. 6 : 1,2. But whoever reads these scriptures, with an impartial mind, must at once perceive that they have no reference whatever to the rite of confirmation, as understood and

Such is a very brief outline of the order and worship of the primitive churches. Simple in their organization and government; pure in doctrine and

practiced at the present day. In the first passage, it is said ' that Peter and John went down to Samaria, and prayed and laid their hands on those whom Philip had baptized *that they might receive the Holy Ghost*, i. e., his miraculous gifts. But what has this to do with the modern rite of confirmation ? Have bishops power, by prayer and the laying on of their hands,' to communicate miraculous gifts ? If not, they might as well stretch themselves upon the dead body of a child, in imitation of Elisha ; or make ointment with spittle for the cure of the blind, in imitation of our Savior ; or anoint the sick with oil, in imitation of the Apostolic Elders ; as pray and lay their hands on those who were baptized, in imitation of Peter and John, who did this to the Samaritan converts, that they might receive the miraculous gifts of the Holy Ghost.' I say *miraculous gifts*,—such as prophesying, speaking with tongues and the like—because they were something visible and obvious to sense; something that struck the wonder and ambition of the wicked sorcerer ; for it is said, *when* Simon saw that through laying on of the Apostles' hands the Holy Ghost was given, he offered them money. Besides, as Dr. Whitby justly observes, if they laid not their hands on *all* that were baptized, it makes nothing for confirmation ; if they did, then Simon Magus also was confirmed and received the Holy Ghost, which it is presumed, the advocates of this rite will not admit. (Letters on Dissent, p. 44.)

That the same thing is meant by the laying on of hands by Paul, Acts 19 : 6. is expressly asserted ; the *Holy Ghost came on them, and they spake with tongues and prophesied.*

As to Heb. vi. 1, 2. the ablest and best commentators agree that the laying on of hands in this passage denotes the same thing as in the passages above referred to—that is, the communication of miraculous gifts. Thus Owen, Whitby, Scott, Rosenmuller, and Stuart.

4

practice ; unincumbered with rites and ceremonies of human invention ; not divided into different sects and denominations ; but all known by the same name and holding the same views of truth and duty ; no Methodists, no Baptists, no Episcopalians, no Presbyterians or Congregationalists, but all christians, united to one another in the bonds of a common faith and of the purest affection, and all devoted in body, soul, and spirit, to the cause of their common Savior and the good of mankind,—truly, these were happy days for the church ; and glorious were her triumphs in extending the dominion of her King, and sending abroad among the nations the tidings of salvation.   The heathen beheld with astonishment these societies of holy men and women, and cried out with admiration—Behold how they love one another. "We are," says Tertullian, one of the earliest and ablest apologists of the christians, "we are ready to die for each other, and we call one another brethren, because we acknowledge one and the same God, the Father, and have been sanctified by the same Holy Spirit, and have been brought from the same state of ignorance to the light of the same marvellous truth."   But, alas ! how soon did the gold become dim and the most fine gold changed ! Long before the close of the second century, the simplicity and purity of primitive times began to be obscured and corrupted by the innovations of men'; and before the commencement of the fourth, a deplorable depravation of doctrine, discipline and morals, had crept into the church and disfigured the body of Christ. Corruption and decay continued to advance, till the sun that rose over Judea, and at first spread so glorious a light among the nations, set in a long, dreary night of a thousand years, and the profoundest darkness, interrupted only by here and there a glimmering of light, settled over the whole world. But the same sun rose again at the Reformation; since which time, it has been on the ascendant, pouring an increasing effulgence over the earth, and shedding a diviner lustre upon the churches of our Lord Jesus Christ. A portion of this celestial light has fallen on the ancient and venerable churches of New-England, to a consideration of which, I shall invite you in my next Lecture.

LECTURE II.

ORIGIN, PRINCIPLES, AND INFLUENCE OF THE CONGREGATIONAL CHURCHES OF NEW ENGLAND.

JEREMIAH vi. 16.

THUS SAITH THE LORD, STAND YE IN THE WAYS AND SEE, AND ASK FOR THE OLD PATHS, WHERE IS THE GOOD WAY, AND WALK THEREIN, AND YE SHALL FIND REST FOR YOUR SOULS.

THE object of the present Lecture is to trace the origin, exhibit the principles, and illustrate the influence, of the Congregational Churches of New England.

These churches, then, are not to be regarded as novel institutions, known only in modern times. They are rather the revival of the churches, that were planted in the earliest and best days of christianity. The immediate agents of this revival were a society of christians in the north of England, who in 1602, separated from the established church, and 'entered into a covenant to study the scriptures, as the only rule of religion, rejecting all human inventions and walking in all the ways of the Lord, made known

4*

or to be made known to them, according to the best of their endeavors, *whatever it might cost them.*'*

This holy purpose was formed in troublous times; and the execution of it cost the venerated founders of these churches incredible hardship and suffering. Popery had indeed received its death blow in England, in the reign of Henry the eighth. But its corrupt and persecuting principles were so inwrought into the very texture of society, and so combined with all the civil and religious institutions of the country, that for nearly a century and a half, they maintained a fierce and bloody conflict with the rights of conscience and the dearest hopes of man. During the reign of Edward the sixth, the reformation made rapid advances. But by a mysterious providence, that wise and pious prince died at the early age of sixteen; and by his untimely death, all the noble designs of reformation, which he is said to have formed, were at once blasted. Mary succeeded,—who was a bigoted papist, and of course, a bitter enemy of reform. Popery was immediately restored in all its abominations, and the reformers, who about this time received the name of puritans, were persecuted with relentless cruelty. At the accession of Elizabeth, in 1558, the fires of Smithfield

* Prince's New England Chronology, p. 4.

were quenched, and the power of Rome restrained. But the reformation instead of advancing, during her reign, went back. Though professedly a protestant, she was in heart more than half a papist. Toleration was a virtue unknown to her thoughts, and abhorrent to her feelings; and though she restored the reformed liturgy of Edward, it was not without making many alterations in it for the worse, and establishing, anew, many of the absurd and unscriptural ceremonies of popery. Nor can any thing better be said of James, and the two Charles's who succeeded Elizabeth.* During their successive reigns, conformity to the established church, in all its rights and forms, was pressed with the greatest rigor, and non-compliance punished with extreme severity. All those ministers who wished for a thorough reformation in the church, and sought to have its doctrines and ceremonies strictly conformed to the scriptures, were treated with the greatest indignity and oppres-

* James had been bred a presbyterian; he had publicly declared that the kirk of Scotland was the purest church in the world, and that the English liturgy sounded in his ears like *an ill mumbled mass*. But on his accession to the English crown, he renounced these sentiments, and affirmed that a Scottish presbytery agrees as well with monarchy, as God and the devil. No bishop, no king, was the argument with which he silenced every plea on the part of the puritans for toleration.—(Grahame's Hist. of the United States, vol. i, p. 215.)

sion. They were driven from their pulpits, deprived of their livings, thrown into prison, and subjected to penalties due only to the vilest of criminals. In this manner, during the reign of Elizabeth, a fourth part of the ministers were suspended as puritans, among whom were the best preachers in the kingdom, at a time when not more than one minister in six could compose a sermon.* And in the second year of Charles the second, two thousand more were compelled to resign their livings, because they could not swear their unfeigned assent and consent to every thing contained in the Book of Common Prayer. The great LOCKE, styles these two thousand ejected ministers, learned, pious, orthodox divines; and when it is recollected that among them were such men as CALAMY, BATES, OWEN, BAXTER, and HOWE, we may well believe, what is said of them by a historian of those times, that their equals have not been seen in any age or nation.

It was in such times, that was nourished that vigorous and manly piety, which led our ancestors to forsake all for Christ, and to turn their eyes towards other lands, where they might enjoy those rights of conscience, that were denied them in the land of their birth. In an address on the subject of removal,

* Hist. of Dissenters, vol. i, p. 60.

they say, " The sun shines as pleasantly on America, as on England, and the Sun of Righteousness, much more clearly. We are treated here in a manner which forfeits all claim upon our affection. The church of England has added to the ceremonies and habits of popery, the only marks of antichrist which were wanting—corruption of doctrine and a bloody persecution of the saints. Let us remove whither the providence of God calls, and make that our country, which will afford what is dearer than property or life, the liberty of worshipping God in the way which appears to us most conducive to our eternal well being·"*

In the spirit of these sentiments, the little company of faithful men, who, in 1602, had formed themselves into a church in the northern counties of England, resolved upon leaving the land of their nativity, where they could no longer be allowed to worship God according to the dictates of his word. Accordingly in 1607, they removed to Amsterdam, and the year following to Leyden. There, with the learned and pious Robinson, for their pastor, they dwelt together in great peace and harmony about twelve years. But Leyden was no place for effecting the great purpose of their association, which was to

* Hist. of Dissenters, vol. i, p. 82.

establish churches in conformity with the word of God ; to transmit evangelical purity in doctrine, worship and discipline, with civil and religious liberty, to their posterity and the world.   Among other reasons assigned for wishing to leave their retreat in Holland, they mention this as prominent :—" An inward zeal, and great hope of laying some foundation, or making way for propagating the kingdom of Christ to the remote ends of the earth ; though they should *be as stepping stones to others.*"   This was the grand object for which God raised them up, and which, by the aids of his grace, they were enabled to achieve.   After repeated seasons of fasting and prayer to engage the blessing of God on their enterprize, the pious exiles, bidding adieu to the land that had kindly received them as strangers and sojourners, prepared to embark for the land of their future destinies.   It was agreed that the elder and largest part of the congregation should remain behind, whilst the younger and more vigorous portion of it should go before, to prepare for them a place in the wilderness.   Among these was the revered Brewster, the noble Carver, and Bradford, and Allerton, and Standish, and a hundred others, prepared like Abraham of old, to go forth at the bidding of God, not knowing whither they should go.   Assembled with their brethren on the broad strand at Delft Haven, their beloved pastor, like Paul, knelt down with them on the sea shore, and with strong crying and tears, commended them to the God who ruleth the winds and the waves. They then embraced and wept in each others arms, till the wind and the tide compelling them to part, they were received on board the ship in waiting for them, and commenced their voyage to the new world, bearing hither the ark of God, and the elements of a mighty empire.*

The various fortunes that attended them, during a long and boisterous passage, I need not enumerate. Suffice it to say, that on the 22d of Dec. 1620, they planted their feet on the rock of Plymouth, and laid the foundation of those civil and religious institutions, which, for two centuries, have been the glory of our land, and the admiration of all lands.

* The Speedwell, of 60 tons, had been purchased in Holland. In this vessel, they came to Southampton, where the Mayflower of 'nine score tons' was, which had been hired for the voyage. In these two vessels they sailed from Southampton the 5th of August, 1620. They had not sailed far, when the Speedwell became leaky. They put into Dartmouth and refitted, and sailed again; but the Speedwell, after sailing about 100 leagues, became so leaky that it was necessary to return. Both vessels went back to Plymouth, where the Speedwell was abandoned; and as many as could be, were taken from her on board the Mayflower, making one hundred and one in all. The rest went back to London. —(Davis' New-England Memorial, p. 28–38.

I have been thus particular in tracing the history of this little band of pilgrims, because they are to be regarded as the primary and chief founders of the New-England churches. And it is worthy of remark, that these first New-England colonists, retaining the principles of their beloved ROBINSON,* always mani-

* The following noble sentiments, with which Mr. ROBINSON concluded his last discourse to the pilgrims before their departure for America, are worthy to be held in everlasting remembrance. To do justice to them, we must remember, that such a spirit of christian liberality as they breathe, was then hardly known in the world.

Brethren, said he, we are now quickly to part from one another, and whether I may ever live to see your faces on earth any more, the God of heaven only knows; but whether the Lord has appointed that or no, I charge you before God, and his blessed angels, that you follow me no farther than you have seen me follow the Lord Jesus Christ. If God reveal any thing to you by any other instrument of his, be as ready to receive it, as ever you were to receive any truth by my ministry; for I am verily persuaded, I am very confident, the Lord has more truth yet to break forth out of his holy word. For my part, I cannot sufficiently bewail the condition of the reformed churches, who are come to a period in religion, and will go, at present, no farther than the instruments of their reformation. The Lutherans cannot be drawn to go beyond what Luther saw; whatever part of his good will, our God has revealed to Calvin, they will rather die than embrace it; and the Calvinists, you see, stick fast where they were left by that great man of God, who yet saw not all things.

This is a misery much to be lamented; for though they were burning and shining lights in their times, yet they penetrated not into the whole counsel of God; but were they now living, would be as willing to embrace farther light, as that which they first received. I beseech you remember it, 'tis an article of your church

fested a spirit of christian forbearance towards other denominations; nor is it known that they, or the Independents in England, to which denomination they belonged, ever oppressed or persecuted any of their fellow-men, on account of their religious sentiments— a fact as honorable to their principles, as it was singular in the age in which they lived.*

covenant, that you be ready to receive whatever truth shall be made known to you from the written word of God. Remember *that*, and every other article of your sacred covenant. But I must herewith exhort you to take heed what you receive as truth. Examine it, consider it, and compare it with other scriptures of truth, before you receive it; for 'tis not possible the christian world should come so lately out of anti-christian darkness, and that perfection of knowledge should break forth at once. And I would wish you, by all means, to close with the godly people of England; study union with them in all things, wherein you can have it without sin, rather than in the least measure to affect a division or separation from them."—(*Mather's Magnalia*, p. 59, 60.

These sentiments, Mr. Robinson recommended to esteem, by exemplifying, in his life and demeanor, the fruits of that Spirit by whose teaching they were communicated; by a character, in which the most eminent faculties, and the highest attainments, were absorbed by the predominating power of a solemn, affectionate piety. He died in Holland, 1625.

* In 1641, the Plymouth colony passed an ordinance in these words: "No injunction shall be put on any church, or church member, as to doctrine, worship, or discipline, whether for substance or circumstance, beside the command of the Bible."

It is the true glory of the Independents, that 'of all christian sects, it was the first, which, during its prosperity as well as its adversity, always adopted the principle of toleration.'—(*Hume's Hist.*, vol. 7, p. 20.

5

Conformity to the ceremonies of the established church being still urged by the adherents of the hierarchy with unabated rigor, multitudes followed their brethren across the Atlantic, that they might share with them in the enjoyment of civil rights and religious privileges.

In the summer of 1630, no less than fifteen hundred persons landed in the new world ; and during the twelve years of Archbishop LAUD's administration, four thousand planters and more than seventy ministers emigrated to America.   Persons of all ranks, ministers and their congregations, driven out by the proscriptions of a bigoted prelate, and an arbitrary king, 'kept sometimes dropping,' says Cotton Mather, 'sometimes flocking into New-England.'   In twenty seven years from the first plantation of the colonies, forty-three churches were formed ; and in the same number of succeeding years, eighty churches more rose into existence.*   All these were Congregational churches.   They were formed after the model of the Plymouth church, and were composed almost entirely of exiles from England, who were ejected from the establishment, because they could not, in conscience, conform to rites and ceremonies prescribed by human authority.

* History of Dissenters, vol. 2, p. 430.

II. Let us now examine the principles on which these churches were founded.

I. In the first place, then, it was adopted, in these churches, as a fundamental principle, that 'the inspired scriptures *only*, contain the true religion ; especially that nothing is to be accounted the Protestant religion, but what is taught in them ; and that every man has a right of judging for himself; of trying doctrines by them, and of worshipping according to his apprehension of the meaning of them.' This, I say, was a *fundamental* principle in the formation of the New-England churches, and constituted, indeed, the grand line of demarcation between them, and the church of England, from which they separated.   For while our fathers maintained that the scriptures were the only and sufficient guide in matters of religion, it was constantly assumed by the advocates of the hierarchy, that the king and bishops had a right to enact cannons, to prescribe ceremonies and forms of worship, and to *enforce conformity by penal statutes*.   This, for more than a hundred and fifty years, was the great subject of dispute between the dominant party in the church of England and our Puritan ancestors, and the chief cause of the sufferings to which the latter were subjected.   Hence, when they came to establish churches in this western world, they formed them on the great principle that ' the Bible, the Bible alone contains the religion of Protestants,' and that Jehovah alone is the Lord of conscience.

2. In respect to faith, they believed the doctrinal articles of the church of England to be agreeable to the scriptures.   While in their native land, suffering for non-conformity, our fathers never complained of the doctrinal part of the Thirty-Nine articles as unsound or unscriptural.   They never had any controversy with the established church on this subject. It was for other and far different reasons, that they refused submission to her cannons, and separated from her communion ; it was because they could not swear to the conscientious observance of rites and ceremonies which were the very refuse of popery ; it was because they were compelled to receive into communion with the church, men of profane and wicked lives, and were forbidden to exercise discipline over them ; it was because Bancroft and Laud, instead of Cranmer and Abbot, wore the episcopal crown, and the intolerant James had said in his star chamber, ' let not puritans be countenanced,' and they were compelled, by royal and prelatical authority, to encourage the profanation of the Lord's day,

by publishing Sunday sports from their pulpits;*—these were the causes of the separation of our fathers from the established church, and not any disbelief or dislike of her doctrines, as contained in the Thirty-nine Articles. These articles, drawn up by the first English reformers, who were in familiar correspondence with the great Calvin, and afterwards revised by Knox and other Scotch reformers, do unquestionably contain the leading doctrines of the Bible and of the Reformation. They were always so regarded by our fathers, who cordially embraced them, as accordant with the inspired oracles, and made them the basis of the creeds and confessions of faith which were introduced into the first churches of New-England.

3. Our fathers came here, smarting from under the rod of ecclesiastical domination. They were, therefore, specially careful to guard the *independence* of the churches. Each church was regarded as a distinct community, independent of all foreign control, and having in itself full power to choose its own officers, enact its own laws, and to regulate all its internal concerns. At first, most of the churches had a pastor and teacher, with two or more deacons. In some churches, ruling elders were appointed.

* Neal's Hist. of the Puritans, vol. 2, p. 265—269.

5*

But this class of officers was not considered essential to the organization of a church, and the appointment of them was after a time discontinued. The officers, thus placed over the church by their own free election and choice, had no arbitrary or imposing power; but maintained government and discipline with the consent and concurrence of the brotherhood. The supreme power was always regarded as being in the assembled fraternity, or in the whole body of christians, composing the church. In cases of difficulty, councils of neighboring pastors and delegates from the churches, were called in to assist in the settlement of them; but their decisions were only advisory; having no *binding* authority over the parties concerned. Such councils are, to the present day, the only ecclesiastical tribunals acknowledged in the churches of Massachusetts. In Connecticut, they have been superseded by Consociations. These are bodies composed of the pastors and delegates of churches within given districts. They have no original jurisdiction over the churches, but form stated tribunals of appeal, advice and decision, in such cases as may be brought before them; and from the experience of more than a century, have been found to exert a most efficient and happy influence in maintaining the purity and peace of our churches.

4. It was a principle adopted in all the first churches of New-England, that none were to be received into their communion, but such as " were sound in the faith, without scandal in their lives, and in the judgment of charity persons of visible holiness." Says governor Winslow, " As the churches of Christ are all saints by calling, so we desire to see the grace of God shining in all we admit into church fellowship, and keep off such as openly wallow in the mire of their sins ; that neither the holy things of God, nor the communion of saints be thereby leavened or polluted." And by one of the earliest and brightest lights of New-England it is added, " that it was adopted as a universal and fundamental maxim, that churches are bound in duty, to inquire not only into the knowledge and orthodoxy, but into the spiritual state of those whom they receive into full communion. And to omit inquiries as to the spiritual experience of those who come to the table of the Lord, has a tendency to fill the sanctuary with those who never had any experimental knowledge of the things of God."* *This* principle, that particular churches ought to consist only of regenerate persons, the letting go of which, as Dr. Owen says, brought in the great apostacy of the christian church, was

* Magnalia, Vol. 2. p. 56–9.

sacredly regarded in all the first churches of New-England; nor to this day has it been renounced by any, but such as have also renounced the spirit and doctrines of those churches, and gone over to the side of heresy.

5. In regard to christians of other denominations, the Congregational churches of New-England act on the principle of open communion; making evidence of christian character the only condition of fellowship.*   Hence, while our fathers admitted

---

* Speaking of the founders of our churches, Governor Winslow says, "They are entirely of the same faith with the reformed churches in Europe, only in church government they are endeavorous after a reformation *more thorough than what is in many of them; yet without any uncharitable separation from them.* He gives instances of their admitting to communion among them the communicants of the French, the Dutch, and the Scotch churches, merely by virtue of their being so; and says, We ever placed a large difference between those that grounded their practice on the word of God, though differing from us in the exposition and understanding of it, and those that hated such reformers and reformation, and went on in anti-christian opposition to it, and persecution of it."   Mather's Mag. vol. 1 : 58.

In the covenant adopted by the Third, now Old South Church in Boston, at its formation in 1669, is the following article, which breathes a spirit of true christian liberality : "We do hereby covenant and promise, through the help of the same grace, to hold, promote, and maintain fellowship and communion *with all the churches of saints,* in all those holy ways of order, appointed between them by our Lord Jesus, to the utmost, especially with those among whom the Lord hath set us; that the Lord may be

that the doctrinal articles of the church of England, and also of the reformed churches of Scotland, Ireland, France, the Palatinate, Geneva, Switzerland, and the United Provinces, were, in all essential points, agreeable to the sacred oracles ; they freely allowed to all the pious members of these churches, fellowship and communion with themselves.*   And in the articles of agreement adopted by the Presbyterians and Congregationalists in England in 1690, and recommended to the churches of Connecticut by the convention of ministers and delegates met at Saybrook in 1708, this broad principle of communion is recognized—" As to what appertains to soundness of judgment in matters of faith, we deem it sufficient that a church acknowledge the scriptures to be the word of God, the perfect and only rule of faith and practice, and own either the doctrinal part of the articles of the church of England, or the confession, or catechisms, shorter or larger, compiled by the Assembly at Westminster, or the confession agreed on at the Savoy, to be agreeable to that rule.†

one, and his name one, in all these churches, throughout all gene. rations, to his eternal glory in Christ Jesus." Hist. of the Old South Church, p. 16.

* Prince's New England Chronology, p. 91.

† Ratio Disciplinæ, p. 310.

6. In conducting public worship, our fathers rejected a prescribed ritual and forms of prayer, not because they considered them unlawful, or forbidden in the scriptures, but because they considered them inexpedient, and not conductive to the great purpose of social worship. They felt, that to be tied down to a liturgy would be a restraint upon their devotions, chilling their affections, and stinting their desires and their petitions. They chose therefore to worship God in the free, unembarrassed manner of the primitive christians, 'not reading their prayers from a book,' but uttering them from full, united and warm hearts.

7. There is another feature in our ecclesiastical polity which I must not pass unnoticed. It relates to the manner in which the independence and purity of the churches are secured, in consistency with the rights and privileges of the congregation. These two bodies are in some respects united and one, but in others, are distinct, independent corporations. In the call and settlement of a minister, which is the great business they have to transact together, each exerts a separate and uncontrolled agency. And yet the concurrence of each is indispensable to the validity of their respective acts. The church has no power to place a minister over the congregation,

nor has the congregation any power to place a minister over the church. In effecting the settlement of a pastor the concurrent voice of the church and society is essential. This is an admirable arrangement. While it secures the church from all improper and dangerous interference on the part of the society, it also secures the society, in the enjoyment of its own rights and privileges, while co-operating with the church, in the settlement and support of a minister. And as each exerts a distinct agency in this matter, and shares alike in the services of the pastor, the effect is to excite in each a mutual interest in the pastor, and in all the concerns of the society of which each forms a component part.

Such, my friends, is a brief view of the polity of the Congregational churches of New-England. Such are the principles of religious liberty, for ' which our fathers suffered in England, traversed the ocean, and sought a dangerous retreat in these remote and savage deserts, that here they might fully enjoy them, and leave them to their latest posterity.'

III. Permit me next to call your attention to the influence which these churches have exerted over the character and institutions of this community. Here let it be recollected, that the first settlers of a country always give character to that country.

Their institutions and habits, whatever they are, usually descend to their posterity, and have a powerful influence in deciding their presesent and future destiny.

Let it be recollected, moreover, that for nearly a hundred years after the settlement of New England, there were very few of any denomination in the land, besides Congregationalists. In 1700, there were in all the New England States then settled, nine hundred Episcopalians, of whom one hundred and eighty five were communicants. There were no Methodists ; and with the exception of Rhode Island, very few Baptists. Not a single church of this denomination existed in Connecticut, and but two or three in Massachusetts. There were at the same time one hundred and twenty Congregational churches in New England, besides thirty churches composed of Indians.* It is plain, then, that New England *is,* what it is, chiefly from the influence of the Congregationalists, and of Congregational principles. I state this with no feeling of boasting, nor with any wish to detract from the merits, of other denominations ; but because it is a fact, and ought to be known. Let us consider this influence,

* Hist. of Dissenters vol. 2, p. 449.

1. In respect to *civil liberty*. The New Testament is emphatically a republican book. It sanctions no privileged orders; it gives no exclusive rights. All, who imbibe its spirit and obey its precepts, are recognized as equals; children of the same Father; brethren and sisters in Christ, and heirs to a common inheritance. In the spirit of these kind and endearing relations, the first christians formed themselves into little republican communities, acknowledging no head but Jesus Christ, and regulating all their concerns by mutual consultation and a popular vote of the brotherhood. In these distinct and independent societies was realized for the first time in this world the perfect idea of civil and religious liberty.

It is true they were not associated for civil purposes; nor did the circumstances of the age allow them to form themselves into a body politic, in which they might enjoy and exercise the rights of free men. Still the *spirit*, the *idea* of the thing was in their minds; and had they been permitted to establish a constitution of civil government, it would unquestionably have been based on the truest principles of liberty.

The Puritans imbibed the same spirit, and derived their principles from the same pure source of light,

6

of holiness and freedom.   They modelled their
churches after the primitive form, and founded them
on the basis of entire independence and perfect
equality of rights.   Twice in their native land had
they saved the British constitution from being crush-
ed by the usurpations of the Stuarts ; and Hume,
who was never backward to reproach both their
character and their principles, is compelled to
acknowledge that what of liberty breathes in that
constitution is to be ascribed to the influence of the
Puritans.*   These were the men who settled New-
England.   They came here bearing in their bosoms
the sacred love of liberty and religion ; and ere they
left the little bark that had borne them across the
ocean, they formed themselves 'into a civil body
politic,' having for its basis this fundamental principle, that they *should be ruled by the majority.*   Here
is brought out the grand idea of a free, elective gov-

---

* " So absolute indeed was the authority of the crown, that the
precious spark of liberty had been kindled and was preserved by
the Puritans ; and it was to this sect whose principles appear so
frivolous, and habits so rediculous, that the English owe the
whole freedom of their constitution." *Hume's Eng.,* *vol.* 5, *p.* 183.

Again, " It was only during the next generation that the noble
principles of liberty took root, and spreading themselves under
the shelter of Puritanical absurdities became fashionable among
the people." *Ibid. p.* 469.

ernment. Here is the germ of that tree of liberty which now rears its lofty top to the heavens, spreading its branches over the length and breadth of our land and under whose shade twelve millions of freemen are reposing. The spirit of all our free, civil and religious institutions, was in the breasts of our pilgrim fathers. It was cherished and invigorated amidst the toils and sufferings which they endured in their native land. It nerved them with courage, and inspired them with hope amid the perils of the deep and the trials of the wilderness ; and prompted and guided their counsels, in founding their churches and establishing a government on principles of the purest republicanism. It was taught by them in the family, in the school, in the sanctuary, and in the hall of legislation. It breathed in their devotions, it animated their efforts, and sustained them in all their self-denials, and hardships and sufferings. It descended to their children in their successive generations, increasing constantly in vigor and strength, till it broke out in the revolutionary war, and was embodied in that excellent form of government, which, while it blesses with equal rights and privileges the millions of our own land, is sending forth a redeeming, emancipating influence among the more numerous millions of other lands, who are groaning under the yoke of oppression and tyranny.

When I think of this, the conviction of my own mind is irresistible, that no men were ever commissioned of heaven to perform a greater, or more noble work than the fathers of New England. They lived not for a day, but for all time and eternity ; not for themselves, but for posterity and the world. Friends of liberty themselves, they were the commissioned heralds and establishers of it in these ends of the earth. The great lesson that man, by the grace God, is capable of governing himself without the scourge of kings, or the dictation of spiritual lords, they had learnt in the school of Christ, and reduced to practice in the churches of Christ. This prepared them to carry the same principles into the establishment of their civil institutions. As in their sanctuaries they could not and would not acknowledge the authority of popes, or cardinals, or bishops ; so when freed from the oppression of foreign nations, and left to choose for themselves, they could not and would not acknowledge the authority of autocrats or kings. The principles which governed them in the formaation of their churches, they incorporated into their civil government ; and all who embrace those prin-

ciples, in the true spirit of them, must, and will
be the decided friends of civil and religious liberty.

2. Let us next consider the influence of these
churches on the *intelligence* of this community. The
primitive churches, from their earliest organization,
took all possible care to accustom their children to
the study of the scriptures, and to instruct them in
the doctrines of their holy religion. For this purpose schools were every where erected, and the
means of common education diffused among all
classes belonging to these christian communities.
Higher seminaries were also erected, in which persons of riper years were instructed in the different
branches both of human learning and sacred erudi-
tion, and youths of suitable qualifications were
trained up for the holy ministry.* The *cause* of this
pious care in the primitive christians for the education of their children was *their ardent love of the
scriptures, and the firm belief they had, that a knowledge of them is an essential means of salvation.*
They wished to educate their children because they
wished their children to be saved.

The same cause operated in the bosoms of our fathers, and prompted them to the same course of con-

* Mosheim, vol. 1, p. 100.

6*

duct. They esteemed the Bible the richest gift of heaven; and themselves, prizing the knowledge of its sacred truths above all earthly treasure, they felt it to be a duty of primary importance to impart the inestimable boon to their offspring, by furnishing them with the means of general education. But for this, our system of free schools had probably never come into existence. The whole system, with all its countless blessings, sprung from the high esteem which our fathers had of the scriptures, and the ardent desire they felt to impart the knowledge of them to their children and to all posterity. Hence, on their arrival in this wilderness, they had scarcely felled the trees and cleared a spot on which to erect their humble dwellings, when they began to counsel, to legislate and provide for the education of the rising generation. Among their earliest laws are to be found those that relate to the instruction of the young in religion and useful learning. Within eight years after the settlement of Massachusetts, Harvard College was founded, and in a very short period, the system of free schools, which has ever since been the glory and defence of New-England, was in full operation. The system was at that time a perfect novelty on earth. Nothing like it, on a large scale, had ever been witnessed. Since that time it has spread into many states of the Union. It was early introduced into Scotland,* Switzerland and Holland—countries by the way, that had embraced the same great principles of the reformation which were held and brought here by our fathers. But even now, in the country from which the pilgrims came, the system is unknown in practice. And only ten years ago, when Mr. Brougham presented a plan to Parliament, to provide by law, for the education of the poor, the representatives of the three kingdoms listened to him with astonishment and delight, as the advocate of new and important principles, though, in fact, he advanced no principles, and presented no plan, but such as are familiar to all our children, and have been in operation in New-England, for nearly two centuries.†

I will only add under this head, that as our fathers were the warm and active friends of edu-

* It was not however till 1696, that the scheme of extending the means of instruction to the poorer classes in Scotland was rendered effectual, by what has well been styled, "one of the last and best acts of the Scottish Parliament."

†It is said that in England, not more than *one child in fifteen* possesses the means of being taught to read and write ; in Wales, *one in twenty;* in France, until lately, where some improvement has been made, not more than one in thirty five. In New-England every child possesses such means. (Webster's discourse on the landing of the Pilgrims.)

cation, so also have been their descendants. The Congregationalists have always been the advocates of a learned ministry, and of the diffusion of intelligence among the people. For this purpose they have, from time to time, made large appropriations of money, both as individuals and as a community. Of the eleven Colleges in New-England, eight were founded and have been mainly supported by the Congregationalists, to say nothing of the Academies and Theological Seminaries that have grown up under their care. The happy effects of this liberal patronage of literature and science, are felt throughout our whole land. In no community on earth is knowledge so generally diffused as in New-England; and *from* no community, equally numerous, have there gone forth so many men to bless their country and the world by their talents, their learning and their piety. We must notice,

3. The influence of these churches on the *morals of this community*. That the first planters of New-England were men of the purest morals, admits of no question. The magistrates of Leyden, speaking of the congregation under the pastoral care of the excellent Robinson, bear this honorable testimony to their character—" These Englishmen have lived among us now these twelve years, yet we never had

one suit or action come against them." Equally evident is it, that the second generation after the settlement of the country, were hardly less distinguished for strictness of morals and general integrity of character. An eminent minister, speaking of this period of our history, in a sermon before the British Parliament, said—"I have lived in a country seven years, and all that time, I never heard one profane oath, and never saw a man drunk in that land." And though after this, there was a gradual departure from the strictness of primitive manners, still it is unquestionably true, that for more than a hundred years after the settlement of the country, the morals of the people were singularly pure and correct. No where has there been so little intemperance, profaneness, and sabbath-breaking; no where, so little of theft, and fraud, and violence; no where, such general obedience to good laws, or such security of person and property, or such uniform regard to justice and truth, and the duties of benevolence and charity, as there was in New-England, during the period of its history, which preceded the old French war. Cases of gross immorality and wickedness did, no doubt, exist; but I speak of the mass of the people, and I feel confident that no person, acquainted with the subject, will be disposed to call in question the cor-

rectness of what I have now said.   Nor at the present time, greatly degenerated as they are, will the
morals of the people of New-England suffer by a
comparison with those of any part of our country,
and, I may add, of the world.   And though the state-
ment made before the British Foreign School Society,
by the Hon. Mr. Barbour, lately our Minister to
Great Britain, may be a little colored, it is still worth
repeating in this place, as it shows the opinion which
disinterested and intelligent men entertain of this
portion of our country.   His words are these :—
" There is not, on the whole face of the civilized
globe, a population more truly moral and religious.
Indeed, we may say of it, that every man was
educated, and every man virtuous ; and that the
exceptions to both were very rare."

What now is the cause of this pre-eminence in morals, for which New-England has been, and is still, so
distinguished ?   The seeds of it were planted by our
pious ancestors in their earliest civil and religious institutions, and in the manners and habits which they
impressed upon their immediate descendants.   And
the churches, planted by their piety and care, have
served as nurseries, in which those seeds have, from
generation to generation, been nurtured and matured ;
and the ripe fruits of which have been spread abroad

over the whole community. All classes of society have felt the moral, healthful influence of these churches. As a general fact, they have been composed of persons of correct sentiments and religious character. The families connected with them, have, to a great extent, been families of prayer, accustomed to read the Bible, to keep the Sabbath, and to train up their children in the nurture and admonition of the Lord.

I do not forget the lamentable defection of a part of these churches in Massachusetts. But with the exception of these, which, compared with the whole, are a very small number, it is an undoubted fact, that the great body of the Congregational churches of New-England have, from the first, maintained the fundamental principles of the gospel, and have exerted a very powerful influence in giving tone and elevation to the morals of the community.

It is customary, I know, at the present day, to inveigh against the doctrines held by our fathers and taught in their churches, as 'austere,' and 'speculative,' and 'demoralizing' in their influence. Our reply is, look at facts. The tree is known by its fruit. And if you reject the doctrines of the New-England churches, as false, or unfriendly to sound morals, then, I insist, that you explain how it is, that this same New-England is so 'signalized by the moral glory that sits on the aspect of her general population'? If Calvinism 'vitiates and corrupts' the habits of a people, how comes it to pass, that in the portion of our country 'where there is the most Calvinism, there is the least crime'? The moral education of this community, let it be remembered, was completed, and its general character formed, before any other denomination existed here,—was completed and formed, therefore, under the influence of the doctrines of the Puritans, which were decidedly Calvinistic. And yet, where is the community to be found, more distinguished for the purity and elevation of its moral sentiments and moral character?

I might appeal, also, to Protestant Switzerland,* to Holland, to Scotland, to the English Non-conformists, and the Protestants of the north of Ireland,— communities that have been distinguished for the Calvinism of their creeds,—and if you call in question the truth, or the moral tendency of those creeds, I call upon you to point me to other communities,

* For an account of the present lamentable state of morals and religion in Switzerland, especially, Geneva, see Christian Spectator, for March and June, 1830—also, Spirit of the Pilgrims, for March, 1830. It is understood, that Unitarianism is now, and has, for a long time, been the dominant religion of the country.

holding other creeds, that can endure comparison with these, in the tone and vigor of their morality.*

4. I must advert to the influence of these churches on the *religious character* of this community. To say that the fathers of New-England were christians, is scanty praise. They were *eminent* christians ; such as the world has rarely seen. They came here in the faith and hopes of the gospel, which they loved better than life ; and here they labored, and prayed, and suffered, that they might found churches, in which that gospel might be maintained in purity and power, and its glory be spread abroad over the face of the whole land. Nor did they labor in vain. The little church, borne to these shores in 1620, in the Mayflower, ' of a forlorn hope,' has multiplied and extended its principles and its polity, till now there are in New-England, more than 1050 churches holding the doctrines of the pilgrims, numbering over 120,000 communicants ; to say nothing of the hundreds of churches, and thousands of communicants, that have gone out from this home of our fathers, and are established in different states of the Union. That all the members of these christian societies are pious, is not pretended. That the great body of them *are*, cannot reasonably be questioned ; and the

* See Edinburgh Review, vol. 36, p. 257.

influence which they exert, in maintaining and diffusing through the community the power of godliness,
is great and most happy.　From the first, they have
been signalized by oft repeated and powerful revivals
of religion.　There never has been a period, of any
considerable continuance, since the settlement of the
country, in which the effusions of the Spirit did not
descend upon some of the churches; while at some
periods, hundreds of them have been visited at once,
and thousands of renewed and joyful converts have
been gathered into their communion.　As the fruits
of these precious seasons of 'refreshing from the
presence of the Lord,' there have always been in the
churches a goodly number of lively, active, devoted
christians—christians who worshipped God in their
closets, in their families, and in the sanctuary; christians who revered the word, the day, and the ordinances of God, and whose hearts and hands were
opened to aid, by their charities and efforts, to send
the gospel to the destitute.　If these things furnish
any evidence of piety, then has piety dwelt and
operated in the Congregational churches of New-
England, and it dwells and operates in them still.
Their influence has been primary and prompt in
most of the benevolent operations of the day.　They
took the lead in the cause of Home Missions.　Their

agency was first and chief in the formation of the American Board for Foreign Missions ; in the formation of the American Education Society; and of the American Tract Society ; and of the American Temperance Society; and they have exerted, at least, their share of influence, in sustaining the operations of the American Colonization and Bible Societies. Their Missionaries are far away in the western wilderness, among the ill-fated Indians, and the destitute whites ; beyond the Mississippi and the Arkansas ; they are to be found in the Islands of the Pacific, at Ceylon, at Bombay, in Greece, at Malta, and along the shores of the Levant. These heralds of the cross, proclaiming salvation to thousands sitting in the region and shadow of death, are the sons of the pilgrims, sent forth and supported by the sons of the pilgrims. Nor will they, we trust, ever desist from the great work of mercy, till the truths of the gospel and the principles of civil and religious liberty, in the defence of which, the pilgrims labored, and suffered, and died, shall be proclaimed in every land, and a guilty, bleeding, dying world, feel their redeeming influence, and break forth into songs of praise and salvation.

And now in conclusion, I cannot forbear to ask, are there here no marks, that God regards these churches with approbation and favor ? The picture I have drawn is not for boasting. I am not insensible to the many and great imperfections and sins, which exist in the churches of my own denomination. I have surveyed them ; and as I surveyed, have been ready to sit down and weep over them. But conceding all, on the score of faults, which can reasonably be demanded, I may still ask, are there here no indications, that the Lord Jehovah looketh down from heaven upon the churches planted by the pilgrims with approbation and favor ? Where is truth, where is piety, where is hope and salvation to be found, if not in these christian societies, which, for two hundred years, have shared so signally in the protection and care of Almighty God, and which, for the same period, have exerted so happy an influence on all the dearest interests and hopes of this favored community ? Shall we be told after all this, that our churches are no churches ; that our ministry is ' unauthorized,' and our ordinances ' invalid,' and that we are all out of the ' appointed' way to heaven, and have no hope but in the 'uncovenanted mercies of God ?' Can those who advance these pretensions, and claim to be the only true Apostolic church, exhibit better evidence of being built upon the foundation of the Apostles and Prophets, Jesus

Christ being the chief corner stone ? Is there in that church which assumes to be in the only 'true line of succession,' to possess the only 'authorized ministry,' and the only 'valid ordinances,' more of humility, and prayerfulness ; more of personal and family religion ; more of self-denial and separation from the world ; more of benevolent concern for the salvation of sinners, and of readiness to make sacrifices to send the Bible and missionaries to the dying millions of the heathen world, than is to be found in hundreds and thousands of churches which she declares to be 'schismatical,' and charges with 'obstinately contemning the means which God has appointed for salvation, and as guilty of rebellion against their Almighty Lawgiver and Judge'.* If it be so indeed that the Episcopal is the only true church, we ask for the signs of it,—signs in a holier and more effective ministry, in a holier and more spiritual communion, and in a greater number of the fruits of conversion and holy living ? If these signs appear, we concede the pre-eminence she claims ; and ask to be received within her favored inclosure. But if they appear not, then let not claims that are based only on spiritual pride and airy forms, be placed in competition with truth and holiness ; or urged

* Bishop Hobart's Companion for the Altar.

7*

to the casting out of the church of God, thousands and millions of those, who love the Lord Jesus Christ in sincerity and in truth.*

But I forbear.   Let us, my brethren, imbibe and cherish the true spirit of Congregationalism ; the spirit of civil and religious liberty ; the spirit of kindness and charity towards all who call on the name of the Lord.   And let us hope and pray, that, as we now extend the hand of fellowship to all of whatever denomination who love the Saviour, so the time may soon come when they shall be disposed to reciprocate the token, and regard us as fellow disciples with them of the same Master, and fellow heirs of the same inheritance.

* These closing paragraphs may seem severe.   Let them not be misapplied.   They are aimed only against *high church notions*. Those who disclaim such notions, and show a spirit of christian liberality towards their brethren of other denominations, have no concern in them.   To all such, of whatever name, let grace be multiplied.

LECTURE III.

DEDUCTIONS FROM THE FOREGOING LECTURES.

JEREMIAH vi. 16.

THUS SAITH THE LORD, STAND YE IN THE WAYS AND SEE, AND ASK FOR THE OLD PATHS, WHERE IS THE GOOD WAY, AND WALK THEREIN, AND YE SHALL FIND REST FOR YOUR SOULS.

In the two preceding Lectures, I endeavored, first, to present an outline of the constitution and order of the primitive churches; and secondly, to trace the origin, principles and influence of the Congregational churches of New-England. Without attempting a review of the train of thought pursued in those lectures, my present object is, to call your attention to several reflections, which naturally arise from the preceding discussion.

1. In the first place, then, there is a striking resemblance between the Congregational churches of New-England, and the churches which existed in the primitive ages of christianity. This fact you must all have noticed, as we passed in review the constitution and polity of these respective churches. It is, no doubt, true, as Dr. Campbell* remarks,

* Lect. on Eccl. Hist. p. 129.

" that there is not a church now in the world, which
is on the model of that formed by the Apostles.
The circumstances of men and things are perpetually
varying, in respect of laws, civil polity, customs and
manners; these, in every society give rise to new
regulations, arrangements and ceremonies; these
again insensibly introduce changes in the relations of
different ranks and classes of men to one another;
exalting some and depressing others."

The church of God has in every age, felt the influence of these changes in society; and in its external
form and modes of worship, has been modified in ac-
commodation to the varying circumstances and habits
of men. But though there are no churches in modern
times exactly on the model of the primitive churches,
still some churches bear a nearer resemblance to
them than others; and this distinction, I am persuaded, can be claimed by the churches of no other
denomination, more justly, than those planted by the
fathers of New-England. Their great object in
coming to this land was to set up the tabernacle of
God, to form churches, and establish a mode of worship and discipline after the manner, which appeared
to them most nearly conformed to the example of the
New Testament. Says Governor Winslow, " The
primitive churches in the Apostolic age, are the only

pattern which the churches of Christ in New England have in their eye—not following Luther, Calvin, Knox, Ainsworth, Robinson, Ames, or any other, further than they followed Christ and his Apostles." Similar language is to be found in the writings of all the New England fathers; and how nearly, in establishing their churches, they were enabled to conform to the divine pattern proposed for their imitation, must be obvious to all who will candidly make the comparison.

The primitive churches, as we have seen, were voluntary associations of pious persons, accustomed to meet together in the same place, for the purpose of social worship, and a mutual participation in the ordinances and privileges of the gospel. They were distinct, independent communities, joined together by no other ties than those of a common faith and a common interest; acknowledging no head but Jesus Christ; each having in itself a perfect right, in obedience to his word, to choose its own officers, to enact its own laws, to exercise discipline over its members, and to adopt whatever regulations seemed best calculated to promote personal holiness and the advancement of Christ's cause on earth. The organization and mode of worship adopted in these christian societies were extremely simple. They had only two classes of permanent officers, elders and deacons. Both were chosen by the free suffrages of the brotherhood, and were set apart to their office by the simplest rites—by prayer and the imposition of hands by the presbytery, or council of neighboring elders. Among the elders or bishops, thus chosen and ordained, there was no assumption of power or pre-eminence, one above another. They were all of the same order, invested with the same authority, and appointed to the same duties; and surrounded as they were by a body of affectionate, confiding disciples, who looked up to them for instruction and guidance, they lived and taught and prayed among them, not as lords over God's heritage, but as helpers of their faith and joy.

The rites practised in the primitive churches, were few and simple; administered in the plainest manner, and with no appearance whatever of show and parade. Baptism was regarded, simply, as the instituted rite of initiation into the christian church; and the Lord's Supper, as the appointed memorial of the death of Christ. No mysterious efficacy, no pretended charm, no incomprehensible power to regenerate and save men, was ascribed to these ordinances, as administered by a particular class of men. All was plain and intelligible, appealing directly to the under-

standing and the heart. The same simplicity characterized the whole worship of the primitive churches.
In their places of meeting, which were an 'upper
room,' a private house, a cave, or a wilderness, there
were no paintings, no images, no burning of incense,
or sprinkling of holy water; no priests with their
mitres, and robes, and other 'paraphernalia of pontif-
ical dignity.' When the christians belonging to a
particular church met for worship, they began by an
invocation of the divine blessing; then a portion of
scripture was read; then the assembly united in a
song of praise; then the elder or presiding officer,
or some other person at his request, rose and addressed them, usually from the portion of scripture read,
and closed with offering a prayer, not from a book
or form, but from the feelings of a warm and full
heart; the people standing the while, and joining
in the prayer, not by responses, but in the silent
assent and pious aspirations of their own minds.

In all these particulars, how striking is the resemblance between the churches, planted by the Apostles, and those established in this land by our venerated fathers? Well may we believe them, when
they say, that the primitive, Apostolic churches, were
the only pattern they had in their eye, in organizing
the churches of New-England. They certainly well

understood their pattern, and were singularly happy in imitating it. And though we may not infer, from the resemblance of our churches to those of primitive times, that our's are the *only true* churches, yet may we justly regard that resemblance as a high recommendation of them, and as furnishing substantial ground for the preference we feel for the order and worship of our own denomination. Especially, have we just cause for preferring that *simplicity* which characterizes the worship in our churches. Simplicity was the grand distinguishing feature in the worship of the primitive churches. It was introduced into them by Christ and his Apostles, as best adapted to the great ends of religious worship—purity of heart and holiness of life ; and the more strictly we adhere to primitive simplicity in the duties and offices of religion, the greater will be its power in the work of sanctification, and the more abundant the fruits of holy living.

2. The principles and polity of the Congregational churches, are happily adapted to all the various circumstances of men, and to the most advanced state of society and the church ; such, as we have reason to hope, will exist during the millennium. That this character belonged to the primitive churches, will readily be admitted. Simple in their organization

and modes of worship, entirely removed from all connexion with civil government, and aiming only to persuade men to lead quiet and holy lives, they were fitted to exist in any state of society, and under any form of government ; and were equally well adapted to the circumstances of the rich and the poor, the learned and the ignorant, the high and the low.

In point of fact, they did exist and flourish in extremely different states of society, and under very different forms of government. They gathered into their communion, men of every grade of intellect, and of the most opposite characters, from the stupid idolater, to the Jewish priest ; from the ignorant peasant, to the sage philosopher ; from the beggar in the street, to the prince on the throne. Many of all these various classes were brought into the fold of Christ, under the ministry of the Apostles and their immediate successors ; and by the simple forms of instruction and worship, which then prevailed in the church, were nourished up unto eternal life. And had those same simple forms been retained in the church, they would have been perfectly adapted to all the exigencies of society, and the varying circumstances of men from that time to the present. The primitive worship demanded no costly sacrifices;

8

it imposed no unmeaning rites; it encouraged no pomp or show; it set up no mere forms or observances as terms of communion. It appealed, not to the senses, nor to the imagination, but directly to the heart and conscience; to the understanding and judgment; to the *common, immutable principles of our nature;* and was therefore equally well adapted to all men, in all circumstances, and of every variety of age and character.

The polity and worship of the Congregational churches are of the same general character. They are plain, simple, intelligible, and, like the gospel whence they are derived, are adapted to no particular age or class of men, but to *man as man,* in all the variety of circumstances in which he may exist. Mere forms and ceremonies are regarded as comparatively, of little importance. The kingdom of God is not considered as consisting in ' meats and drinks,' or in ' divers washings' and ' carnal ordinances'; but in 'righteousness, peace, and joy in the Holy Ghost.' The great point aimed at in Congregationalism is to fit men for this kingdom and form in them this temper; and the means, which are deemed best adapted to this end, are the exhibition of divine truth, and the administration of divine ordinances, in the plainest and simplest forms. Hence every thing like parade and show, every thing that is addressed merely to the imagination and senses, is rejected from our worship, as unfavorable to spiritual devotion, and fitted rather to obstruct, than promote the due impression of God's truth and ordinances. In short, the Congregational mode of worship, like that which prevailed in primitive times, addresses itself to the *intelligence*, to the *consciences* and *the hearts of men*, and is therefore likely to be most highly prized and relished, where there is the most intelligence and the most pure and spiritual affection. Let society advance to ever so high a degree of knowledge and refinement, and let true religion prevail in the same degree, and if any thing can be inferred with certainty, from the genius of the gospel, or the principles of the human mind, there can be no doubt that the simple, unadorned forms of worship, adopted in our churches, would be most happily adapted to the exigencies of such a state of society, and wisely calculated to cherish and promote the spirit of holiness.

At the same time, such is the truly liberal and catholic spirit, which characterizes the principles of Congregationalism, that if the millennium were to commence to-morrow, there would be no need of modifying or changing any one of those principles.

It sets up no exclusive terms of communion ; it insists upon no outward forms, or unessential rites as conditions of christian fellowship.   It receives *all*, whom there is evidence to believe Christ has received.   On this ground, our churches, without relinquishing or altering any one principle of their organization, or polity, might admit to their communion the whole world, converted to Christ, and extend the hand of fellowship to *all* christians of whatever name or denomination.   But on the principle of the Episcopalians, the millennium can never come till the whole world become Episcopalians, and on the principle of the Baptists, the millennium can never come, till the whole world become Baptists ; and on the principle of the Papists, the millennium can never come till the whole world become Papists ; but on the principle of the Congregationalists, the millennium may come at any time, and they be prepared to enter into the spirit of it, and embrace in the arms of christian fellowship, all who love the Lord Jesus Christ in sincerity and truth, however much they might differ in certain points of form and ceremony.   And such difference will doubtless exist in the purest and best days of the church.   The unity which Christ prayed might exist among his friends, and which, we may be sure, *will* ultimately exist among them, is not a unity in outward forms, or in things unessential to salvation ; but it is a unity of faith in the fundamental doctrines of the gospel, and of love, towards all who possess the temper and bear the image of Christ. This is a unity that is practicable and highly important. It was delightfully exemplified in the primitive christians, who, while they differed on points of form and ceremony, some observing and others rejecting many of the rites of Judaism, still loved one another as brethren and communed as fellow christians. It is now exemplified by many individual christians in different denominations, and especially by the missionaries among the heathen. These devoted servants of God, whether Episcopalians, Baptists, Methodists, Congregationalists, or Presbyterians, in their love for Christ and the souls of men, rise above the little prejudices of sect and name ; and abhorring the bigotry that erects into terms of communion, mere points of external order, are accustomed, as they have opportunity, to unite with one another in commemorating the love of their common Lord and Savior, and in all the offices of christian fellowship and affection. This is only an exemplification of what will every where be witnessed in the latter day glory of the church. Christians will then, I

8*

cannot doubt, have their peculiar preferences and attachments in respect to modes of worship and rules of order. To expect all men to think alike in such things is as unreasonable as to expect them to look alike. But such things will then be regarded in their true light, as comparatively little things,—certainly not as lines of division among christians ; and all of whatever denomination loving the Lord Jesus Christ, and his truth and cause with supreme affection, will love and embrace one another in the bonds of holy fellowship aad communion. And what is this, but the universal extension of the principle now adopted and acted upon in the Congregational churches of New England, that of opening the door of communion to all who love the Lord Jesus Christ.

3. The polity of the Congregational churches is wisely adapted to the genius of our civil institutions. This might at once be inferred from the fact, that these institutions originated from the same spirit, and were established by the same men, that were employed in establishing our churches. They are, indeed, but distinct parts of one grand harmonious system of civil and religious liberty. Both are pervaded by the same spirit, and are based on the same principles of freedom. It is the distinguishing characteristic of our civil institutions that they are

elective. They originate in the choice of the people. With the people is the primary source of power. They have the right to elect their own rulers, and through them to enact their own laws, and to adopt whatever measures are deemed best calculated to promote the general good.

Precisely similar is the constitution of our churches. No man, or body of men, has any power to preside over, or govern them independently of their choice. They are essentially free communities, possessing and exercising the right of choosing their own officers and regulating their own concerns, responsible to none but Jesus Christ, the sovereign Head of the church. In common with the members of civil society, the members of any particular church have a right to delegate power to individuals of their body for certain purposes ; and also to associate with other churches, if this is thought best, for the greater security of their common interests. But all this is mere matter of choice, decided always by the voice of the majority, and is thus in exact harmony with the spirit of our civil institutions.

I must add further, that such are the organization and order of our churches, that they tend, directly and powerfully, to strengthen and perpetuate our civil institutions. Every Congregational church is not only a school of divine knowledge and piety, but also of civil and religious liberty. *There* is cherished the spirit, and *there* are taught the principles which lie at the foundation of a free government. It is impossible that persons, who are accustomed in the church, to feel and act as freemen, should be the friends of arbitrary power. As in matters of religion they have been taught to call no man master; so in matters of civil government, they will submit to no authority but that which is lawfully and freely constituted over them. Equally impossible is it, that such persons, I mean those who are actuated by the true spirit and principles of Congregationalism, should ever wish for a union between church and state. They know full well that the only tendency of such a union is to destroy both civil and religious liberty, and to produce, either an ecclesiastical or political despotism, both of which are equally to be dreaded. And though the remark may seem needless, in this place, I will just drop it in passing, that notwithstanding all the clamor that is raised by infidels and others against the Congregationalists and Presbyterians, as wishing to bring about a union between church and state, there is no denomination in the land that more sincerely deprecates such a union; and none would have to forfeit greater privileges, or make greater sacrifices, if it should finally be effected.

4. The principles and polity adopted in Congregational churches, are well calculated to secure their purity, both in doctrine and practice. It is held as a fundamental principle in these churches, that the Bible is the only rule of faith and worship, and that every man has a right to study the scriptures and judge of their meaning for himself. The doctrines taught in these churches are, and with some slight variations, have been from the first, decidedly evangelical ; and they have been, and are now, with some few exceptions, preached with great purity and effect. In every church, personal piety, grounded on a change of heart, and exemplified in a christian life, is required as an indispensable qualification for membership. Each church, also, has the right, and is in duty bound, to watch over its members, and to advise, reprove, or exclude from communion, as the case may be, such as walk disorderly, or violate their covenant engagements. The ministry is also carefully guarded. Before any one can receive license to preach the gospel, he must produce a certificate of christian character, and of regular membership in some church of Christ, and undergo an examination, both as to his doctrinal and experimental acquaint-

ance with religion, before an association of ministers. At the time of his ordination he is again examined, and if after settlement, he departs from the faith, or becomes immoral in conduct, he is amenable, either to the church of which he is pastor, or to the association to which he belongs, who have a right to dismiss and depose him.

The practical influence of these principles has been found, from experience, to be eminently happy. For more than two centuries, they have secured to the churches of New-England, unparallelled prosperity and great unanimity in doctrine and practice. Whilst they recognise the Bible as the only rule of religion, and encourage all desirable freedom of inquiry, they guard the churches against corruption and error, by shutting the door of their communion against the admission of unworthy members, and the door of the ministry against the intrusion of unsanctified and heretical teachers.

It is, indeed, often urged, as a serious objection against the order of our churches, that they have no uniform confession of faith, or formulary of doctrine, to which their ministers and members are required to give their assent ; and in this particular, it is claimed, that the Episcopal church has greatly the advantage. Our reply is, look at facts. There are in New-England, about 1200 churches of the Congregational order. Of these, more than 1050 are decidedly orthodox ; leaving less than 150, chiefly in Massachusetts, that have renounced the doctrines of the Reformation, and become Unitarian. In Connecticut, there are 220 Congregational churches, all of which, with the exception of one, are evangelical, and are under the pastoral care of evangelical ministers, so far as they have ministers of any kind. These facts are important. They furnish very decisive evidence of the efficacy of our ecclesiastical polity, to preserve the purity of the churches ; and in view of them, we cannot forbear to ask, whether that church, which boasts of its liturgy and articles, as being the great safeguard against corruption and error, can furnish better evidence of unity in faith, and purity in doctrine and practice ?

That the liturgy and doctrinal articles of the Episcopal church, are substantially correct in sentiment, is readily admitted. Nor are we disposed to deny that, in some respects, they may exert a favorable influence in guarding the faith and purity of the church. But, when they are set forth as the grand preservative from error, and a superiority is claimed for them in this particular, above the polity and worship of every other denomination, I must pause

and examine, before I can admit the validity of such
claims.   What, then, are the facts in the case ?
The Thirty-nine Articles, we admit, are, for the
substance of them, agreeable to the scriptures ; they
are decidedly evangelical ; and every minister officiating in the Episcopal church, is required to give
his unfeigned assent and consent to them.   But does
it hence follow, that all the clergy in that church,
are evangelical in doctrine, or united in sentiment ?
This is so far from being the fact, that of the eleven
or twelve thousand ministers belonging to the established church in England, only two or three thousand
are considered as evangelical.*   Three-fourths, at
least, of the whole number, differ entirely in sentiment, from such men as SCOTT, NEWTON, RICHMOND,
and the Editors of the Christian Observer.   In general, they are high churchmen, and decidedly Arminian in sentiment, holding the doctrine of baptismal
regeneration, and of the exclusive validity of the
Episcopal ministry and ordinances, and consigning
all others, not conformed to their church, to the
' uncovenanted mercies of God,' as furnishing for
them, the only hope of salvation.†

* See Hart's Installation Sermon, p. 24.
† The fact is, that subscription to the Thirty-nine Articles, is
not generally regarded in England, (is it in this country ?) as
implying a cordial or *ex animo* belief of them.   They are rather

And how is it in this country? We have the authority of one, whom the Christian Observer* declares to be a "most respectable American Episcopalian clergyman, and distinguished preacher," for saying, "that there is not a party among the ranks of the English clergy, in relation to points of theological discussion, which has not its counterpart in every important particular, among the clergy of America; and that the din and clash of those controversies which excite the most feeling in England, are echoed back by combatants here, who are as eager and obstinate as any in christendom." "Our church," this writer adds, "with the exception of a few particulars, unconnected with theological doctrine, is an exact miniature of yours." I take no pleasure in stating these facts. I simply refer to them, to show, that the high claims set up by our Episcopal brethren, for their Articles and Liturgy, as securing to their church unity of faith, and purity of doctrine and worship, are unfounded. The truth is, very little reliance can be placed on confessions of faith and formularies of doctrine, for preserving the church

considered as 'articles of peace,' in the sense explained by Dr. Paley, in his Moral Philosophy; and thus understood, they can be, and actually are, subscribed by persons of the most opposite sentiments.

* Christian Observer, Nov. 1823.

from false sentiments and corrupt practice. The
best means for effecting this, are the means best
adapted to enkindle and keep alive a spirit of humble, devoted piety.   The reformed churches of
Germany and Switzerland once had, and many of
them now have, a correct creed—scriptural formularies of doctrine, to which all who ministered at the
altar, or came to the communion, were required to
give their assent.   But most of those churches, with
their ministers, have passed through all the various
grades of Arianism, down to the lowest sort of Socinianism, and even Deism, and yet retain the form of
christian churches and the name of christan ministers.
Articles on paper, however scriptural, oppose but a
feeble barrier to irreligion and error, when these are
seated in the heart, or are dominant in the head.
They may, perhaps, enforce an outward submission,
and produce an outward uniformity ; but of what use
are these if error and sin lie lurking beneath ?   In no
country on earth are the forms of popery so rigidly
observed as in Italy ; and yet in no country, are
there so many infidels and atheists.

5. The principles and polity of the Congregational
churches are powerfully influential in promoting
vital godliness. Look back to the primitive churches;
while they retained their simple form and simple

modes of worship, they retained also their spirituality of character. Religion was in the hearts of the disciples a principle of living energy. Christianity mightily prevailed and flourished. The standard of the cross was set up in a thousand lands. Converts were multiplied as drops of the dew. Hundreds and thousands, attracted by the simple majesty of truth, ministered in love and applied by the secret influences of the Holy Spirit, turned from dumb idols to serve the living God. The gospel was then proved to be the power of God unto salvation. Its moral influence, untrammeled by forms and ceremonies of human invention, 'was too mighty for philosophy, priestcraft, arbitrary power and prevailing corruption combined.' But by degrees, primitive simplicity passed away; and in its stead, ceremonies and rites were multiplied almost beyond enumeration. The sacraments were increased from two to seven. Religious worship was encumbered with endless forms and observances, and celebrated with great splendor and show. The ministers of Christ, not contented with being simple teachers of religion, and helpers of the faith and joy of their brethren, began to lord it over God's heritage; to claim pre-eminence one above another, and to aspire after the honors and distinctions of the world. At length, under Constantine, the church became an ally of the state, and christianity the established religion of the empire.   And now the work of decay and corruption went on with melancholy rapidity.   Neither the ordinances nor the doctrines, nor the organization nor the officers of the church were any longer what they had been.   'The houses of worship were made to rival royal palaces; the ministers of the church, divided into different grades, and possessing different powers, were as numerous as the servants of a king, and fared as sumptuously.   Paintings and statues, and gold and silver vessels; various and most costly instruments of music; scarlet and purple and fine linen; robes and mitres and crowns, and all things magnificent and imposing, were employed to give splendor to divine worship, and cause a strong impression to be made on the senses.'   But not to dwell longer on the mournful picture, suffice it to say, that things continued to wax worse and worse, till finally all ecclesiastical, and civil power too, was vested in the pope of Rome; and kings and bishops were alike compelled to do him homage.

Now it is deeply affecting to notice, how at every step, as the church departed from the primitive, simple form of a republic, and assumed, by degrees, first the form of an aristocracy, then of a monarchy, and last of all, of a frightful despotism, piety constantly declined ; the power of religion languished, till at length its light was smothered by the corruptions of popery, and scarcely a single ray interrupted the deep darkness of a thousand years.

Then it was that 'bishops could not write their own names, that Hebrew and Greek were reckoned heretical, that indulgences were sold, that prayers were offered to dead men and women, that priests were thought to have power to forgive sin, that an old man was reckoned the vicar of the Almighty, and the inquisition was armed with its horrible powers, and did its work of blood and desolation.' Religion was utterly lost amidst the multiplied and nameless forms that were thrown around it, and the spirit of devotion expired in a blind and senseless attachment to rites and ceremonies.

But, to return from this digression, which I shall not regret, if it only serve to impress our minds, more deeply, with the importance of adhering, in our worship, to the pure pattern of the gospel.— Religion revived at the Reformation, and throwing off the mummeries of popery, assumed something of its unadorned, primitive simplicity ; and just in proportion as it did this, it prospered and flourished. In Switzerland, Holland, and Scotland, where the

9*

form of church government, and modes of worship, were the most simple, and approached nearest to what they were in primitive times, most of the life and power of religion was exhibited. This is emphatically true of New-England. Here our ecclesiastical order and modes of worship, have, from the first, been characterized by great simplicity. Our churches have had no liturgy, no forms of prayer, no ritual of any kind. In our places of worship, there is nothing of decoration, or splendid ornament, to attract the eye, or please the fancy. Nothing is thought of but the gospel, the prayers, the songs of praise. All is devoid of pomp and show. The minister is clothed in a modest black dress, and his sole business is, to fix the thoughts of the congregation on God, and to instruct them in the things of God. Simplicity and seriousness; thought, intelligence, truth, addressed directly to the understanding and the heart,—these are, and ever have been, the characteristics of divine worship, as performed in the Congregational churches of New-England. The fruits are manifest. A manly and vigorous piety has been maintained in the churches. Their members, to a very great extent, have been exemplary, intelligent, devoted christians. The presence of God has been manifest in their sanctuaries; the influences of the Holy Spirit have descended like the dew of Hermon ; and great multitudes, 'planted here in the house of the Lord,' have been transferred to 'flourish eternally in the courts of our God.' If the tree is known by its fruit, the evidence is decisive, that the simple form of government and mode of worship, that prevail in our churches, are most happily calculated to promote personal piety, and prepare the soul for the purer and nobler worship of the heavenly world.

And here, let me make this general remark, that *just in proportion as christians rise in the tone of their piety, their regard for forms and ceremonics is diminished, and their attachment to simplicity in the worship of God is increased.* On the other hand, *just in proportion as men depart from the spirit of religion, they are wont to substitute forms in its place, and to become bigoted in their attachment to the mere ceremonials of worship.* For an illustration of this, look at the Romish church. The devotees of that communion, can see no truth, or excellence, or piety, in any religion except *theirs.* Theirs is the only true, infallible church ; theirs, the only authorized ministry, and sacraments, and worship ; and all who are without the pale of their church, are without the hope of salvation, and bound over to perdition. In the mean time, their worship is little else than a mere business of the senses ; music, and painting, and pantomime, and shows of various kinds, are made to take the place of the essentials of devotion. Their religion is a mythology ;* every thing grand and impressive and sanctifying in christianity, is turned into mere dramatic, or scenic effect ; simple prayers are superseded by splendid ceremonies ; saints and images are made the intercessors with an almost forgotten God, and the immediate objects of devotion are lost sight of. A relic, a ceremony, a penance, a mere counting of beads, or uttering of prayers in an unknown tongue—these are accounted the great things in religion, the weightier matters of the law ; whilst the love of God and mankind, holy affections and a holy life are regarded as of little worth. No wonder that the populace, that uninformed and worldly men should be pleased and captivated with this system of superstition, which appeals so directly to the senses, and is so well adapted to lull the conscience and sooth the heart in its sins. The true practical effect of the whole sumptuous apparatus of Romish worship is to work upon the natural sensibilities, and to flatter men with a belief that they are the favorites of God, while in

* See Natural History of Enthusiasm, p. 52.

fact they are the slaves of sin. This is the effect of every system of worship, just in proportion as it draws off the mind from the *spirit* of religion to the mere *forms* of it. And it was doubtless with a view. to prevent this effect, and to inspire 'in the bosom a spirit of enlightened, fervent devotion, that our Lord Jesus Christ appointed the worship under the gospel to be simple, spiritual, appealing directly to the intellect and the heart, and fitted to raise the thoughts to God and heaven.

And now if the principles and polity of our churches bear so near a resemblance to the churches of primitive times; if they are adapted to all the various circumstances of men, and to the most advanced state of society and the church; if they harmonize with the genius of our civil institutions and tend directly to strengthen and perpetuate them; if, in fine, they are calculated to secure the purity of the churches, to promote personal, religion, to form a character of intelligent, fruitful piety, and thus qualify us to serve God here and to enjoy him hereafter; if this is the nature and tendency of the principles of Congregationalism, then have we good reason for strong attachment to them, and for wishing to see them extended through the world, and perpetuated to the latest posterity. They are principles, my friends, which are connected with all the best interests of society, and the dearest hopes of men. To publish and extend them on earth, Apostles and Martyrs labored, and suffered, and died. To establish and perpetuate them in this land, our venerated fathers left the land of their birth, traversed the ocean, dwelt in the wilderness, and here laid down their lives a sacrifice in the cause of civil and religious liberty.

The blessings resulting from these principles we enjoy in rich abundance, and on us is devolved the high responsibility of transmitting them to those who shall come after us. And while I would call upon all to cherish an enlightened attachment to the liberty wherewith Christ hath made us free, and to guard, with the influence of their united prayers and efforts, the sacred trust committed to their keeping, let me enforce the exhortation by rehearsing the words of two* of the venerable fathers of New England, uttered by them just before they ascended to their reward in heaven. " We do earnestly testify,' say they, ' that if any who are given to change, do rise up to unhinge the well established churches in this land, it will be the duty and interest of the churches to examine whether the men of this trespass are more

* Rev. John Higginson, and Rev. William Hubbard.

prayerfull, more watchful, more zealous, more patient, more heavenly, more universally conscientious, and harder students and better scholars, and more willing to be informed and advised, than those great and good men who left unto the churches what they now enjoy ; if they be not so, it will be wisdom for the children to forbear pulling down with their own hands the houses of God which were built by their wiser fathers, until they have better satisfaction."

LECTURE IV.

CHARACTER AND VINDICATION OF THE PILGRIMS.

PROVERBS x. 7.

THE MEMORY OF THE JUST IS BLESSED; BUT THE NAME OF THE WICKED SHALL ROT.

Of the truth of this inspired declaration, how interesting an illustration is furnished in the history of the fathers of New-England? Their proud oppressors, with their guilty works, have long since passed into oblivion, or are remembered only with detestation and reproach. But the memory of the pilgrims still endures, fragrant as the breath of the morning ; and the lapse of time, instead of obscuring, only adds fresh lustre to their names, by unfolding, more clearly, the grandeur of their enterprise and the immensity of the blessings conferred by them on their posterity and the world.

Brief, indeed, are the notices of their character and works, that have come down to us, in the annals of our country ; and now, that the winds and storms of two hundred winters have swept over their graves, we look in vain for the places where most of them sleep beneath the silent clod. But they still live ;

10

live in the principles they taught ; in the institutions they established ; in the schools, academies, and colleges, and in the virtue, intelligence, and happiness, which bless their descendants, and make this, in comparison with other lands, as the garden of God. These are the monuments of their fame ; far more durable than sculptured columns, or triumphal arches. They are a living memorial of the wisdom and piety of our fathers, known and read of all men ; and in the recollection of their virtues and their deeds, thousands and millions, yet unborn, will rise up and call them blessed.

Of the causes which drove our ancestors from the land of their birth, and brought them to these shores; of the churches they have founded, and of the influence which these churches have exerted over the interests of this community, some account was given you in a preceding lecture.

My present object is, to furnish you with a brief sketch of the character of our fathers, and also to attempt a vindication of them on some points, where their conduct has been severely censured.

The subject, I am aware, can have little claim to your attention on the score of novelty. It has so often been considered, that it would be vain for me to expect to present it in a new light, or to furnish any thing, either in point of fact, or illustration, that is not already familiar to most of my hearers. And yet, such is the nature of the subject, so strong and deep are its associations with all our dearest privileges and brightest hopes, that it can never fail to interest, to instruct, and to profit, however frequently presented, or however familiar to our thoughts.— The truth is, the founders of New-England were no ordinary men; the purpose for which they lived and died, was no ordinary purpose. They were emphatically the benefactors of mankind; raised up of God, to establish new forms of society, to develop new principles of government, and to open new sources of human happiness and human improvement. Such were their characters and achievements, and so immensely interesting the consequences which have resulted from their principles and conduct, that so long as there remains in us any regard to an illustrious ancestry, any veneration of virtue and piety, any love of civil and religious liberty, we can never speak or hear of the patriarchs of New-England, without feeling that they are most worthy to be held in grateful and everlasting remembrance.

Nearly all nations, of which we have any account, lose their origin in a fabulous antiquity, or in the obscure traditions of a savage state. Even those countries, where the arts and sciences have been most flourishing, were originally planted, or were afterwards overrun by barbarians who had been driven from their homes by the pressure of want, or the love of conquest. But far other causes gave rise to the settlement of New-England. Her origin runs back to no fabled antiquity, is lost in no dark traditions of a barbarous age. Her first foundations were laid in intelligence, in virtue and piety. New-England owes her existence to the love of religion, and solely to the love of religion.* The men who first came here, were the chosen instruments of God, in extending his empire on earth ; and for the accomplishment of this great work, they were eminently qualified. They were not barbarians, whose descendants, like the Greeks and Romans, groped their way to civilization, through ages of superstition and

* The following note from Hutchinson, seems well founded.— " Whether Britain would have had any colonies in America at this day, (1760,) if religion had not been the grand inducement, is doubtful. One hundred and twenty years had passed, from the discovery of the northern continent by the Cabots, without any successful attempt. After repeated attempts had failed, it seems less probable that any should undertake in such an affair, than it would have been if no attempt had been made.—*Hutch. Hist. p.* 11. It required the patience, the self-denial and fortitude of the pilgrims, to endure the labors and surmount the difficulties of planting a colony on these bleak and inhospitable shores.

darkness. They were not pagans, like the first inhabitants of Great Britain, to whom christian missionaries were sent, to turn them from dumb idols to the living God. They were not papists, who, like the planters of South America, shut up the word of God from their posterity, and entailed upon them the bondage of a corrupt and superstitious religion. They were not slaves, who came here to toil in the service of despotism, and transmit to a debased posterity, their own sad inheritance. They were not a band of lawless adventurers, fleeing from the hand of justice, and coming here only for purposes of conquest and aggrandizement. They were *enlightened freemen*, who understood the nature, and appreciated the blessings of liberty. They were *devoted christians*, who, not being permitted to worship God according to the directions of his word, in their own land, fled to this American wilderness, that they might organize churches, and institute modes of worship, in accordance with the example of the Bible. They were, in short, men of great decision and firmness of character ; of untiring patience and dauntless fortitude, and withal, ardently attached to the gospel and its institutions, ready to make any sacrifices in its defence and propagation, and qualified to

10*

lay broad and deep the foundations of a mighty empire.*

About to make this country the theatre of signal displays of divine mercy, the great Husbandman brought hither the choicest vine. "He sifted three kingdoms that he might plant the American wilderness with the finest wheat;" and the glorious harvest now waves over a thousand lands. But this is a general view. Let us descend to a few particulars.

In the first place, then, the fathers of New-England were men of *strong intelligence,* and of

---

* The coarse jest has often been repeated by foreign writers, that the Adam and Eve of the colonies came out of Newgate; and even Dr. Johnson could stoop to utter the malignant remark, that the Americans are a race of convicts, and ought to be thankful for any thing we allow them, short of hanging.—*Boswell, vol.* 2.

And yet the very work, in which the first of these sarcasms is repeated with great complacency, contains the following just sentiment respecting the character of our ancestors.

"There are few states, whose origin on the whole, is so respectable as the American—none whose history is sullied with so few crimes. The Puritans who had fled into Holland to avoid intolerance at home, carried with them English hearts. They could not bear to think that their little community should be absorbed and lost in a foreign nation; they had forsaken their birth place and their family graves; but they loved their country and their mother tongue, and rather than their children should become subjects of another state, and speak another language, they exposed themselves to all the hardships and dangers of colonizing in a savage land. No people on earth may so justly pride themselves on their ancestors as the New-Englanders."—*Quarterly Rev. No.* 4.

great moral fortitude. Many of them were from families of distinction, elevated by rank and fortune, and highly honored in their own country for their talents and learning. Most of the ministers and civilians who came over with the colonists, received their education in the Universities of Oxford and Cambridge; and many of them were deeply versed in the literature and science of the day, especially in the learned languages.* It was no uncommon thing for the early ministers of New-England to read the Hebrew and Greek scriptures, at their ordinary morning and evening devotions in their families. They brought over with them extensive libraries, and were hard students all their lives. New-England has never beheld in her councils men better qualified to lead in the affairs of state, than were Bradford, and Winslow, and Winthrop, and Haynes, and Hopkins, and Bradstreet, and Wyllys. Nor have the churches ever been blessed with more able or learned ministers than were Wilson, and Cotton, and Norton, and Shepard, and Hooker, and Stone. Messrs. Hubbard and Higginson, who personally remembered this class of ministers, describe them in the following terms: " They were men of great

* Ramsay's Colonial Civil History, p. 235. Allen's Biographical Dictionary.

renown in the nation from which the Laudian persecution exiled them. Their learning, their holiness,
their gravity, struck all men who knew them, with
admiration. They were Timothies in their houses,
Chrysostoms in their pulpits, and Augustines in their
disputations." The people who followed these holy
men into the wilderness were their spiritual children,
who imbibed their spirit and sentiments, and loved
and venerated them as their fathers in Christ. They
were men of great enterprize, and of the most decided moral courage. They feared God; and therefore felt and acted as if they had no one else to fear.
In the defence of their principles, they were prepared to make any sacrifices, or to encounter any
dangers. They were men to whom conscience and
duty were every thing; human threats and human
punishments nothing. They could endure shame,
reproach, imprisonment and exile; but they could
not endure to yield up their consciences to the dictation of arbitrary power, or wear the yoke imposed
upon them by the prince and prelates of a corrupt
establishment.

We can, indeed, form no conception of the hardships and sufferings endured by our fathers in
securing for us these pleasant homes and this goodly
inheritance. They were hardships and sufferings,

the bare thought of which, it would seem, must have disheartened and overwhelmed them. And yet they endured them, not only with fortitude, but with cheerful, unrepining resolution. Like the primitive christians, they took joyfully the spoiling of their goods; and were willing to suffer all things for the sake of Christ and his cause. Hence, when the whole scene of their sacrifices and dangers was full in their view, instead of shrinking from them, they could meekly say, "When we are in our graves, it will be all one, whether we have lived in plenty or in penury; whether we have died in a bed of down, or locks of straw. Only this is the advantage of the mean condition, that *it is a more freedom to die.* And the less comfort any have in the things of this world, the more liberty they have to lay up treasure in heaven." When told by their friends in England, that they might perish by the way, or be cut off by famine or the sword, their only reply was, "We may trust God's providence for these things. Either he will keep these evils from us, or will dispose them for our good, and enable us to bear them." The sentiments expressed by one of their number may indeed be taken for the sentiments of all. "I take notice of it, he says, as a great favor of God, not only to preserve my life, but to give me contented-ness in all our straits; insomuch that I do not remember that ever I did wish in my heart, that I had never come into this country, or wish myself back again to my father's house. The Lord Jesus Christ was so plainly held out in the preaching of the gospel, and God's Holy Spirit was pleased to accompany the word with such efficacy to many, that our hearts were taken off from Old England, and set upon heaven. The discourse not only of the aged, but of the youth also, was not, how shall we go to England, but how shall we go to heaven."

Sentiments like these bespeak a moral courage in the men who uttered them,—a spirit of selfdenial and selfdevotion to the cause of God and the good of mankind, which were hardly surpassed in the purest and best days of christianity. They are indeed the 'sentiments of a lofty virtue,' of a high, immovable confidence in God, and well entitle our fathers to be regarded as of kindred spirit with Apostles and martyrs.

We may next notice their *disinterestedness and high public spirit.* Had our fathers been men of a narrow, selfish policy, they would never have left the green fields of England, for the dreary wilds of America. A little bending of the conscience, a little relinquishment of duty, and a slight outward submission to mitred authority, would have kept them in possession of their quiet homes and spared them the sacrifices and perils of a removal into this distant and desert land. But they had higher and nobler views. They had a largeness of heart and a grandeur of purpose which forbad their settling down at home, contented if *they* might but live in ease and die in plenty. Their eye was on other and better objects. They had, as they expressed it, "an inward zeal and great hope of propagating the kingdom of Christ to the remote ends of the earth." This was the grand inspiring motive of their enterprize : they looked beyond the little circle of selfish interest, to the kingdom of God and the salvation of their children, and their fellow men. With this object in view, they bade farewell to their friends and their homes, and the land of their father's sepulchres, and committed themselves to the perils of the deep and the trials of the wilderness. Immediately on their arrival in the place of their future destinies, we behold them, not absorbed, each one, in seeking his own private interests, but dwelling together as a great family, having a common interest, and all endeavoring to promote the general good.* While

* The peculiar situation of the Plymouth colonists naturally led them, like the Virginians, for a time, to throw all their property into

yet the wilderness was unsubdued, and the wild beasts and savages were prowling around their paths, they began to legislate and act for the public weal and the benefit of posterity.*   The sanctuary, the college, the school house, the hall of legislation, and the court of justice, rose nearly at the same time with their own humble dwellings; and whenever a new settlement was commenced, it began and arose under the combined influence of all these causes. At a very early period, a law was passed, obliging all heads of families to teach their children and apprentices so much learning as to enable them to read perfectly the English language.

Within seventeen years after the settlement of Massachusetts, the system of free schools was regu-

a common stock, and like the members of one family, to carry on every work of industry by their joint labor for the public good. This policy was soon found to be attended with great difficulties ; and after a trial of about three years, it was relinquished, and a separation of possessions was introduced, though the full right of separate property was not admitted till a much later period.— *Mather, B. 1 Ch. iii.*

* " After God had carried us safe to New England, say they, and we had builded our houses, provided necessaries for our livelihood, reared convenient places for God's worship, and settled the civil government; one of the next things we longed for, and looked after, was to advance learning and perpetuate it to posterity, dreading to leave an illiterate ministry to the churches, when our present ministers shall be in the dust."—1 *Hist. Collect,* 240.

larly organized, and became matter of legislation.*
Every township of fifty householders, was required
by law to maintain a public school, at public expense ; and every township of one hundred householders, to maintain in like manner, a grammar
school, to instruct youth and fit them for the Univer-
sity, *to the end*, they say, in this memorable law,
*that learning may not be buried in the graves of our
forefathers in church and state.*† Only eight years
after the arrival of our fathers in Massachusetts,
four hundred pounds sterling were granted by the
General Court to found Harvard College. Large
additional grants were soon made, both in land and
money ; and so general was the interest felt in the
prosperity of that Institution, established expressly
' for Christ and his church,' that frequent contributions were made to aid its funds, both in Connecticut
and New-Haven ; and money was granted from the
public treasury.

At the same time, the most *liberal provision* was
made for the support of the gospel. The institutions
of religion were held in such high estimation by our
fathers, and were deemed so essential to the prosperity of society, that they considered it no hardship,

* The system existed in practice several years earlier.
† This was in 1647.

11

but rather a privilege, to contribute of their substance to establish and support them. The first churches in New-England, though their numbers were small, generally poor and subjected to all the dangers and difficulties incident to the settlement of a new country, usually supported two able, experienced ministers. The six first towns in Connecticut enjoyed the constant labor of ten able ministers. This was one minister to about fifty families, or to two hundred and sixty or seventy souls.*

Had the people of the present day as high a regard for the gospel, or were they as willing to make sacrifices for its propagation among the destitute, our country, which is now in danger of becoming a moral waste, would speedily be blessed with the means of salvation, and the teeming millions of its population be saved from barbarism and ruin.

The enlarged and benevolent spirit of our pilgrim fathers, was not confined to the people of their own community. They were men who pitied the heathen ; and one object of their emigration to this country was, that they might diffuse the light of the gospel over this dark and benighted continent.

In the very infancy of the colony, they began to take measures for the civilization and conversion of

* Trumbull, vol. 1, p. 280.

the Indians. Towards these ill-fated sons of the forest, they always conducted with strict justice, and generally, with great kindness and forbearance.* "They did not claim one foot of ground in the country, till they fairly purchased it of the natives."† At a very early period, a school was established at Harvard College, to teach them the rudiments of the christian faith. Missionaries were sent forth to guide them into the way of life, and great was the success which attended their labors. Eliot, the famed Apostle of the Indians, lived to see twenty-four christian societies organized among them, and these instructed by twenty-four native preachers. In 1700, there were thirty Indian churches in New-England, under the pastoral care of the same number of Indian preachers. In some villages, a large proportion of

* Says Dr. Dwight, " the annals of the world cannot furnish a single instance, in which a nation, or any other body politic, has treated its allies, or its subjects, either with more justice, or more humanity, than the New-England colonists treated these people. Exclusively of the country of the Pequods, the inhabitants of Connecticut bought, unless I am deceived, every inch of ground contained within that colony, of its native proprietors. The people of Rhode-Island, Plymouth, Massachusetts, and New-Hampshire, proceeded wholly in the same equitable manner.— Until Philip's war, in 1675, not a single foot of ground in New-England was claimed, or occupied by the colonists on any other score, but that of fair purchase.—*Dwight's Travels, vol.* 1, *p.* 167.

† Mather's Magnalia. History of Dissenters, vol. 2, p. 431,

the families were families of prayer.   In this noble work, Eliot, and Mahew, and Bourne, and Cotton, took the lead, and were followed by Treat, and Sargeant, and Edwards, and Brainerd.   Thousands of poor Indians, gathered into the fold of Christ by the instrumentality of these servants of God, have entered the world of light, and with them are rejoicing in the presence of their common Redeemer and King.

Another trait in the character of our fathers, was their attention to the religious instruction of their children.   They adopted the maxim that 'families are the nurseries of the church and the commonwealth ; ruin families, and you ruin all.'   They aimed, therefore, to engage the presence and blessing of God to abide in their families.   With their own hearts set upon heaven, they were earnestly desirous that their children might be prepared to follow them to the world of glory.   For this purpose, they constantly maintained family religion and family government. The word of God was daily read, and the worship of God daily observed in their houses.   They sought for their children, as they did for themselves, *first* the kingdom of God and his righteousness.   The influence of this principle was prominent in the family, in the school, and in all their domestic and social arrangements. Their towns were churches, so that the young people saw little abroad to weaken the effects of the example and instructions which they enjoyed at home. In the great work of training the young for the service and glory of God, parents and magistrates, and pastors and churches co-operated with mutual zeal and fidelity. These labors, honored with the blessing of God, rendered the second generation of the colonists hardly less distinguished for their piety, than were their fathers. The great body of them were members of the church and adorned their profession by a holy life.

That the fathers of New England were the ardent friends of liberty will not be questioned. They had shown themselves its firmest advocates in their native land ; and when driven out by the rod of oppression, they came here bearing the standard of liberty, and set it up, a glorious ensign to the nations. And that their children might be qualified to live under a free government, and enjoy its blessings, they took great pains to form in them correct moral principles ; and to accustom them, from childhood, to that subordination, and those habits of obedience which are essential to the existence of republican institutions. They carefully inculcated the duty of obeying the laws *for conscience sake*, and of show-

11*

ing respect to superiors, especially to magistrates. And that there might be the best reason for such respect, they chose, with much circumspection, out of all the people, able men, such as feared God and hated covetousness, to bear rule over them. The suffrages of the people were not solicited by needy adventurers, nor intrigued after by young and ignorant ambition. Government was not considered as established for the gratification or emolument of office seekers, but for the protection and happiness of the people ; and promotion was conferred, not *prematurely*, as the reward of patriotic professions, but *wisely*, as the reward of tried integrity in the subordinate grades of usefulness.

Chosen by such a people, and for such purposes, the rulers of the land were a terror to evil doers, and a praise to those who did well. By their talents, their age, their experience, their examples, and their official influence, they upheld religious institutions, sustained the energy of law, gave a healthful tone to public morals and endeavored to prevent crime, and supersede the necessity of punishment, by establishing over the mind the authority of Jehovah. The result was the universal prevalence of moral principle and moral practice, and to a great extent, of true religion. For it pleased God to make it manifest by the blessings

bestowed on our fathers, that godliness is profitable
unto all thing, having promise of the life that now is,
and of that which is to come.

No men ever cherished a more sacred regard for
the Sabbath than did our pilgrim ancestors.*   One
reason why they left Leyden, was the unrestrained
profanation of the Lord's day, by the inhabitants of
the place.   They trembled for the consequences of
such an example to their children, and wished to
remove where the full influence of God's holy day
might operate in forming their characters and fitting
them for heaven.   They considered the Sabbath as
the firmest support of virtue and religion, and, consequently, as lying at the foundation of social happiness
and political prosperity.†   They therefore observed

* " It was a distingishing mark of a Puritan in those times, to
see him going to church twice a day with his Bible under his arm ;
and while others were at plays and interludes, at revels, or walking
in the fields, or at the diversions of bowling, fencing, &c. on the
evening of the Sabbath, *these* with their families were employed in
reading the scriptures, singing psalms, catechising their children,
repeating sermons or prayers.   *Neal, vol.* 1, *p.* 560.

† The sentiment of the excellent Mr. Shepard, minister of Cambridge, was the common sentiment of the day.   " If any state
would reduce the people under it, unto all sorts of superstition
and impiety, let them erect *a dancing Sabbath ;* and if the god of
this world would have all professors enjoy a total immunity
from the love of God, and all manner of licentiousness allowed
them without check of conscience, let him then make *an every*
day Sabbath."   Magnalia, vol. 1, p. 349.

the day with great seriousness.   They prepared for its approach, by a seasonable adjustment of their temporal affairs ; they welcomed its arrival with joy, and spent all its hours in the public and private duties of religion.   A sacred stillness reigned in their habitations, and throughout their villages and towns, well befitting the day of God, and well calculated to raise the affections and thoughts to the eternal rest of heaven.

For the scriptures our fathers cherished the profoundest veneration.   They received them with unhesitating faith, as given by inspiration of God.   They studied them as the only rule of religion, and humbly endeavored to conform their doctrines and lives to this only standard of faith and practice.   What those doctrines were, I have before stated.   They were the doctrines of the Reformation, the doctrines of Grace, the doctrines now denominated Calvinistic, and held in all the evangelical churches of New-England.*   Our fathers believed these doctrines,

---

* It has been suggested that it would be well to omit the above terms in describing the doctrinal belief of our fathers.   But the author can see no good reason for this.   It is true, that the enemies of evangelical religion, and among them some professed ministers of the gospel, are much gratified when, by misrepresentation and perversion, they can make these terms the occasion of bringing reproach upon the doctrines of orthodox christians.

not because they were taught by Luther, or Calvin, or any other uninspired man,—they thought for themselves ; they called no man master,—they believed them, because they found them in the Bible ; and they loved them, because they had felt their power in their own hearts, and had witnessed their effects on the hearts and lives of others. Hence, they embraced them with a deep and thorough conviction of their vital, saving energy. They taught them in their families ; they taught them in their

They intimate that our fathers believed all the doctrines taught by Calvin and Luther, and simply because *they* taught them ; and they would fain have it understood that the orthodox of the present day believe precisely the same doctrines, and on the same ground. They know better ; and when they make such representations, they do it only to bring odium upon a system of doctrine which they dare not attempt to refute by fair argument.

When the doctrines of the Reformation, the doctrines of Grace, the doctrines denominated Calvinistic are spoken of, it is intended to designate a *system* of truth—a system distinct from Arminianism and Socinianism, and which in its *essential principles* was held by the reformers, was held by our fathers, and is now held by evangelical christians in New-England, and throughout the world. It is not pretended, nor by an honest interpretation of language, can it be affirmed, that every sentiment, which may at any time have been attached to this system, has been believed by all who have embraced the system. This is not true ; and those who insinuate to the contrary, *know* it is not true ; and when Unitarians and others represent the Orthodox as holding *all* that Calvin and the reformers taught, there is too much evidence that they do it with a *wicked design*, and may justly be charged with bearing false witness against their neighbors.

schools ; they taught them in their churches ; and their entire characters and habits were formed under their influence.

With what vigilance they guarded the purity of the churches, I have already intimated. They admitted none to membership but such as gave evidence of personal religion ; and they retained none in their communion, who lived in known disobedience to the laws of Christ.

That their churches might be composed of holy persons, their children saved and the cause of religion sustained and promoted in the land, our pious ancestors had their hearts much set upon revivals of religion. They prized above all earthly blessings the influences of the Holy Spirit. It was no doubtful matter with them, whether those influences are a reality, or whether they are indispensable to the conversion of sinners. They hung all their hopes of salvation for themselves and their posterity on the word of God, and the efficacy of his Spirit. Hence, ministers, and magistrates, and churches, were much in the habit of unitedly looking up to God for the effusions of his Spirit. Frequent and special seasons of fasting and prayer were set apart for this purpose ; and most signal were the displays of divine power and mercy which they were permitted to witness. A volume would scarcely contain the instances on record of the special out-porings of the Holy Spirit on the churches of New-England. In 1629, in 1630, and 40, the presence of God was wonderfully manifested in most of the settlements; and, in allusion to these seasons of mercy, one of them says: In those days, God, even our God, did bless New-England.* Says another, alluding to the same seasons of refreshing: Let us call to mind the first glory in the first planting of New-England. O that converting glory which did then appear: multitudes were converted to thee, O Zion. Let me say, multitudes, multitudes were converted to thee, O Hartford, to thee, O New-Haven, and to thee, O Windsor; and the same may be said of many churches in New-England.† I might descend to later times, especially to 1680, to 1705, to 1734, 40, and 45, at which periods, and to some extent during the intervals, God poured out his spirit upon the churches in a very wonderful manner, and thousands of happy converts were gathered into the fold of Christ. But enough has been said to show in what estimation these seasons of divine mercy were held by the fathers of New-England; and how, in answer to

* Gillie's Historical Collections.
† Prince's Christian History, vol. 1, p. 76.

their prayers, showers of grace have, from generation to generation, descended upon this favored portion of our land, clothing it with moral verdure, and rendering it as the garden of God.

If I have not mentioned piety, as forming a distinct trait in the character of our fathers, it is because this trait was blended with all their feelings and actions, and shone forth as the grand, pervading principle of their conduct and lives. Says the Rev. Thomas Prince : " There never was, perhaps, before seen such a body of pious people together on the face of the earth. For those who came over first, came for the sake of religion, and for that pure religion, which was entirely hated by the loose and profane of the world. Their civil and ecclesiastical leaders were exemplary patterns of piety. They encouraged only the virtuous to come with, and follow them. They were so strict on the vicious, both in church and state, that the incorigible could not endure to live in the land, and went back again."

Indeed nothing in the character of these men, especially their ministers, strikes me with such admiration, as their fervent, devoted piety. They were eminently men of God. To know him, to serve him, to enjoy him, was with them the great end of existence. They were mighty in prayer. They were trained in the school of affliction, which gave a deep, mellow tone to their piety; a holy familiarity and fervor to their supplications, and caused them to feel and act habitually as strangers and pilgrims on earth. Their virtues took hold on another world; their graces were matured by suffering, and were daily invigorated by converse with God and invisible scenes. Hence their contempt for external circumstances, their patience in tribulation, their fortitude, their tranquility, their inflexible resolution, their steady hope and lofty purpose. One overpowering sentiment possessed their minds and impelled them onward in the path of duty and heaven, regardless alike of the frowns and flatteries of the world, and of toil, and danger, and suffering;—it was the fear and the love of God, and the hope of his eternal favor in glory. That favor they now enjoy. They rest from their labors and their works do follow them.

II. But it may be asked, had these men no faults? They had,—they had the faults of our common nature; nor were they wholly free from the faults of the age in which they lived; and these, misrepresented and exagerated as they often have been, are regarded by some as almost a complete offset to their virtues and as rendering them worthy only of doubtful praise. Let us examine some of the charges brought against our fathers, and see whether they are capable of vindication.

1. In the first place then, it is alleged that they held the doctrines of Calvin, which are said to be 'gloomy,' 'chilling,' and of 'demoralizing tendency.' Their doctrines were no doubt Calvinistic ; and we rejoice to see these doctrines associated with so much unquestionable excellence of character ; with such strong intelligence, lofty virtue, and nobleness of purpose. It is a circumstance which speaks much for the truth and excellence of these doctrines, and goes far to convict those who bring the objection that they are 'gloomy and severe,' either of gross ignorance, or of wilful misrepresentation. "When other systems shall have produced a piety as devoted, a morality as pure, a patriotism as disinterested, and a state of society as happy, as have prevailed where the doctrines of our fathers have been most prevalent, it may be in season to seek an answer to this objection." At present I will dismiss it by citing the opinion of a learned civilian and infidel, found in the British Encyclopedia.* After an account of the Calvinistic and Arminian systems, to the latter of which he gives the preference, this writer says :

* Article Predestination, said to have been written by Robert Forsyth, Esq.

" There is one remark which we feel ourselves bound to make. It is this that from the earliest ages down to our own days, if we consider the character of the ancient Stoics, the Jewish Essenes, the *modern Calvinists* and Jansenists, compared with that of their antagonists, the Epicurians, the Saducees, the Arminians and the Jesuits, we shall find that they *have excelled, in no small degree, in the practice of the most rigid and respectable virtues ; and have been the highest honor to their own age, and the best models for imitation to every succeeding age.*"

2. Our fathers have been accused of ' superstition,' of ' rigidness' and ' bigotry' in their religious opinions and practices. To this accusation I am not careful to answer ; because it is rarely brought, except by those, who are wont to regard all steadfastness in the faith, and strictness in religion, as superstition and bigotry. Indeed change these terms of reproach, so often cast upon the memory of our fathers, *into piety and constancy in the service of God*, and you will have a much truer representation of their characters, than is usually given of them by their enemies. The ancestors of New England had not learnt, as have many of their descendants, to tamper with their consciences and their God. Religion and eternity were with them serious matters ;

and if in defending the one, and preparing for the other, they were unbending, and sometimes erred, on the score of strictness, it was certainly erring on the safe side, and in a manner which it were wisdom in their posterity to imitate, rather than indulge in that thoughtlessness of God and another world, which is characteristic of so many at the present day.

3. Our fathers have been censured for adopting the laws of Moses as the ground of their own civil code. But this is not true any further than they considered those laws to be of a *moral* nature and adapted to their circumstances. They immediately departed from them, in a great variety of particulars ; and as their circumstances changed, they departed from them still further,—a fact which plainly proves that they never meant to adopt the Mosaic law, as universally binding on themselves or other christians. That they had a high respect for that law, as instituted by God, is true,—that they adopted many of its principles into their own system of regulations is equally true ; and in doing so they acted most wisely. One immediate effect was to diminish the number of human actions punishable by death, from one hundred to fourteen. That in some particulars, they followed the Jewish law too closely is admitted.

Would it have been wiser had they adopted the judicial code of their native land, in which were registered at that time one hundred crimes, the punishment of which was death, and which have since been increased to one hundred and seventy six ?[*]

4. It is alleged that they enacted laws which were oppressive to other denominations, and, moreover, that they were actually guilty of persecution. This indeed is a serious charge, and to some extent must be admitted to be true. And yet whoever candidly examines the facts in the case, will find abundant evidence that our fathers, in this respect, were far from being sinners above all who have dwelt on the earth. Many of the laws that are complained of were enacted when there were few or none of any other denomination in the land. They were designed to protect and support their own ecclesiastical and civil order ; and not to operate at all as persecuting or oppressive enactments against christians belonging to other sects. It is also true that most of those persons who are said to have been persecuted and oppressed, suffered not so much for their religious opinions, as for their offences against the state.[†]

[*] Dwight's Travels, vol. 1, p. 166.

[†] This, according to Winthrop, was the ground of the sentence of banishment, passed on Roger Williams. 'He broached and divulged diverse new opinions against the authority of magistrates,

12*

Some of them outraged all decency and order,
and committed such acts as would unquestionably,

as also wrote letters of defamation both of the magistrates and
churches.'—*Winthrop's Hist. of N. E. edit. by Savage, vol.* 1. *p.* 167.

For a particular account of the causes for which Mr. Williams
was banished, see Hutchinson's History of Massachusetts, vol. 1,
p. 41 ; Dwight's Travels, vol. 1, p. 142 ; Magnalia, vol. 2, p. 430.
As for the laws, subsequently enacted against the Baptists and
Quakers, no one, most certainly, can justify them.   They were
oppressive and wrong.   But let no one reproach, too severely, the
memory of our fathers, in this matter, till he is certain, that *in
similar circumstances*, he would have shown a better temper.

It is allowed that they were culpable ; but we do not concede,
that in the present instance, they stood alone, or that they mer-
ited all the censure bestowed on them.   " Laws similar to those of
Massachusetts were passed elsewhere against the Quakers and
also against the Baptists, particularly in Virginia.   If no execution took place here, it was not owing to the moderation of the
church." *Jefferson, Virg. Query, XVIII.*

" The prevalent opinion among most sects of christians, at that
day, that toleration is sinful, ought to be remembered ; nor should
it be forgotten that the first Quakers in New England, beside
speaking and writing what was deemed blasphemous, reviled
magistrates and ministers, and disturbed religious assemblies ;
and that the tendency of their opinions and practices was to the
subversion of the commonwealth in the period of its infancy."
Holmes's Amer. Annals.   Hutch. vol. 1, *p.* 180—9 .

" It should be added, that in Massacuusetts the law which
enacted that all Quakers returning into the state after banishment, should be punished with death, and under which four
persons were executed, met with great, and at first, successful
opposition.   The deputies, who constituted the popular branch of
the legislature, at first rejected it ; but afterwards, on reconsider-
ation, concurred with the magistrates, (by whom it was originally
proposed,) by a majority of one only." *Chr. Spect.* 1830, *p.* 266.

at the present day, subject a man to imprisonment, if not to a severer punishment.

The fathers of New-England, endured incredible hardships in providing for themselves a home in the wilderness ; and to protect themselves in the undisturbed enjoyment of rights, which they had purchased at so dear a rate, they sometimes adopted measures, which, if tried by the more enlightened and liberal views of the present day, must at once be pronounced altogether unjustifiable. But shall they be condemned without mercy for not acting up to principles which were unacknowledged and unknown througout the whole of Christendom ? Shall they alone be held responsible for opinions and conduct which had become sacred by antiquity, and which were common to christians of all other denominations ? Every government then in existence assumed to itself the right to legislate in matters of religion ; and to restrain heresy by penal statutes. This right was claimed by rulers, admitted by subjects, and is sanctioned by the names of Lord Bacon and Montesquieu, and many others equally famed for their talents and learning. It is unjust then, to 'press upon one poor persecuted sect, the sins of all Christendom ?' The fault of our fathers was the fault of the age ; and though this cannot justify, it certainly furnishes an extenuation of their conduct. As well might you condemn them for not understanding the art of navigating by steam, as for not understanding and acting up to the principles of religious toleration. At the same time, it is but just to say, that imperfect as were their views of the rights of conscience, they were nevertheless far in advance of the age to which they belonged; and it is to them more than to any other class of men on earth, the world is indebted for the more rational views that now prevail on the subject of civil and religious liberty.

5. Another accusation, I must notice: the ancestors of New-England, were the dupes of a miserable delusion; they believed in witchcraft, and put several persons to death, who were supposed to be guilty of that crime. But were they alone in this delusion? Has not a belief in witchcraft prevailed in every age of the world, and among all classes of men? Was it not believed in by Lord Coke, by Lord Bacon, by Sir Matthew Hale, and Justice Blackstone. So late as the reign of George the second, there were laws in force in Great Britain, against witches.* It

* Blackstone Comment, Book iv. ch. 4.

The authors of the Universal History, have stated some palliative facts, which deserve to be reported on such authority:—

has been justly observed by an intelligent historian, "that the importance given to the New-England trials, proceeded more from the general panic, than from the number executed ; more having been put to death in a single county in England, in a short space of time, than have suffered in all New-England, from the first settlement to the present time.*

It may be well, also, for those who are accustomed to reproach our fathers, as fanatics, to recollect that leading prelates in the church of England, bishops and archbishops, upon their knees, pronounced king James, a very Solomon for wisdom, not doubting that he spoke by inspiration of God, and that this same Solomon wrote a book to prove to his subjects the reality of witchcraft, and the duty of proceeding against the professors of this black art, with all the severity of the law.†   What, then, is the amount of

"In justice to the ministers and people of New-England, we are to observe, that the persecutions for witchcraft, were carried on by wretches, partly to gratify their private resentments and interests, and partly from a spirit of enthusiasm and credulity ; nor could they have happened, had it not been for the *weakness of the governor*, and Dr. Mather, who were rendered the tools of more designing men.   The people in general, and some ministers, particularly Mr. Caleb, of Boston, detested them, and remonstrated against them from the beginning, but all to no purpose."—*Vol.* 39.

* Hutch. Hist. vol. 2, 15—16.

† History of Dissenters, vol. 2, p. 445.

the charge brought against our ancestors for believing in witchcraft? Why, that they did not at once shake off the errors of the times, and mount, at a single step, into the superior light and advantages of the present day.

But it is time to have done with vindication. The fathers of New-England need it not. Their memorial is before us; it is in their works; in the peace, the plenty and happiness which prevail in this land of the pilgrims; in the virtue, intelligence and enterprize which distinguish the sons and the daughters of the pilgrims; in the schools, the churches and higher seminaries of learning which every where greet the eye, and bring to every hamlet and to the door of every cottage, the means of knowledge and the blessings of salvation; in the numerous charities and institutions for the relief of suffering and want, which adorn and bless this community; in the extension of the blessings of civil and religious freedom throughout our country; and in the prospective extension of these same blessings throughout the world—these are the monuments which proclaim the virtue of our ancestors, and will perpetuate their memory till the end of time. Faults, I admit they had; yet, take them all in all, the world never saw their like. There are men, I know, who can see in the character of our fathers, nothing to claim their gratitude, or their veneration; and who manifest a sort of parricidal pleasure in magnifying and exposing their failings. What in them was great, and disinterested, and generous, and noble, they keep out of sight; and hold up to public view, only what was little, defective and absurd. If in any part of their example, there be any thing unsound, ' these flesh flies' 'detect it with unerring instinct, and dart upon it with a ravenous delight.' I envy them not their pleasure. Let them enjoy it alone. Their taste reveals their temper, and shows them incapable of discerning excellence and worth, when associated with the love of God and a firm faith in the doctrines of his word.

Let us, my friends, ever cherish, in grateful recollection, the memory of our fathers. They are well entitled to our gratitude and veneration. " No sober New-Englander can read the history of his country, without rejoicing that God has caused him to spring from the loins of such ancestors, and given him his birth in a country, whose public concerns were entrusted to their management. There is no account in the annals of colonization, in which the principal actors have left fewer memorials behind them calculated to awaken the regret of mankind, or call forth a blush on the faces of their descendants, or more fitted to command the admiration and applause of both."*

Let us, then, vindicate our claim to so illustrious an ancestry, by always showing ourselves ready to defend their characters, to adhere to their principles, and follow in their footsteps up the bright and shining way to heaven. Let us, on all occasions and at all times, firmly and perseveringly, maintain the spirit and the form of that religion, which was at once, the main-spring of the counsels and the crowning glory of the character and achievements of the pilgrims. The great inheritance, which, with so much toil and suffering and prayer they purchased and bequeathed to us, let us here, in the presence of God, resolve to preserve and bequeath to our children, that so we and they may rise to join the glorious company of our ancestors, who, in long and bright succession, have ascended to the world of light and blessedness.

* Dwight.

LECTURE V.

CAUSES AND EXTENT OF DECLENSION IN THE CONGREGATIONAL CHURCHES OF NEW-ENGLAND.

JEREMIAH, ii. 21.

YET I HAD PLANTED THEE A NOBLE VINE, WHOLLY A RIGHT SEED:
HOW THEN ART THOU TURNED INTO THE DEGENERATE PLANT OF
A STRANGE VINE UNTO ME?

IT has often been remarked, that between the history of the ancient Israelites, and that of the people of New-England, there are many striking points of resemblance. Like them, our pilgrim ancestors were persecuted and oppressed in the land where they dwelt. Like them, they were delivered from the power of their oppressors, by the 'uplifted hand and outstretched arm of Jehovah.' Like them, they were conducted by a gracious Providence through the perils of the sea, and planted, *a noble vine, wholly a right seed,* in the land of their future residence. And like them, their descendants have forsaken the God of their fathers, and are 'turned into the degenerate plant of a strange vine.' To trace the

13

causes and extent of this degeneracy, is the object of the present lecture.

1. In attempting to point out some of the more prominent of these causes, it is necessary to go back to an early period of our history. The first planters of New-England were, with few exceptions, professors of religion. They came here that they might enjoy, unmolested, their religious rights, and establish that form of civil and ecclesiastical order, which they deemed most agreeable to the word of God, and best adapted to promote the interests of his kingdom. Their motives were pure, and their object noble.

But they had not yet learnt the full import of the Savior's declaration—*My kingdom is not of this world*. They knew not how to separate the church from the state. Perhaps they deemed it impracticable; or if not impracticable, wholly inexpedient. Hence, in all their early, public proceedings, there was an unnatural blending of things spiritual with things temporal—a most unhappy and hurtful intermixture of church and state. At the first court of election, held in Massachusetts, 1631, a law was passed that from that time, no persons should be admitted to the freedom of the body politic, but such

as were members of some of the churches within its
limits.*"

Whatever may be said as to the right of the colonists to enact such a law, the extreme impolicy of it
is perfectly obvious.   It is, no doubt, to be regarded
as the first, in a series of causes, which tended to
corrupt the churches, and bring on that declension,
which has since overspread so large a portion of the
land of the pilgrims.   The influence of the law was
especially disastrous in three respects.   " It held out
a sort of premium for hypocricy."   For all who wished to enjoy the privileges of freemen, would of course
determine to become members of the church ; and
as this could be permitted only on a profession of piety, they would be strongly tempted to make such a
profession without the requisite qualifications.

Those, on the other hand, who had too much conscience to do this, or who having applied for admission to the church, were rejected, would of course

* Holmes' Amer. Annals.   This law continued in force till
1662, when, by the remonstrances of Charles the Second, the colonists were compelled to make some alteration in it.   It was enacted that every candidate for the privileges of a freeman should
produce a certificate from the minister of the parish that he was
a person of orthodox principles, and of honest life and conversation.   This alteration of the law was chiefly in appearance.   Its
bad influence was hardly at all diminished.   See Grahame's History of America, I. 263.

be decidedly opposed to the existing order of the churches, and exert all their influence to overthrow it. They deeply felt the privations to which they were subjected ; and as they considered them wholly unjust and oppressive, they loudly complained of them, and as early as 1646, petitioned not only the courts of the colonies, but the British parliament, praying, as they say, in ' behalf of thousands,' that they might enjoy with others the rights and'privileges of freemen.*

In the mean time, the ministers and churches sympathising with this class of men in the disabilities under which they labored, were strongly inclined to extend relief to them.   The proper way of doing this was to abolish the law which they had so unwisely enacted.   But this was deemed sacred.   In these embarrassing circumstances, a powerful temptation was presented to *lower* the terms of admission to the church, and to receive persons to communion on slight and insufficient evidence of piety. The result was, that not a few, as we have reason to believe, were early introduced into the churches,

---

* For a larger discussion of the subject introduced in this lecture, and for several facts stated, see in the Spirit of the Pilgrims for 1829, Letters on the Introduction and Progress of Unitarianism in New-England—a series of very able and useful papers.

who though, in the main, correct in sentiment and moral in conduct, were strangers to the power of godliness, and averse to the duties of strict religion.

Their influence was like an incubus on the vitals of the church. It tended to depress the tone of piety, and to infuse a spirit of formality and worldliness into the services of religion.

The next cause to be specified was the introduction of the *half-way covenant.* This strange anomaly in religion naturally sprung from the law, the mischief of which I have just described. From natural increase and emigration from abroad, the class of persons in the colonies, not qualified to profess religion, soon became numerous, Many of these were highly respectable for their talents and general worth of character; and it was felt to be a hardship, that they should be deprived of the privileges enjoyed by others around them, and especially that they should be denied the right of baptism for their children, which they had always enjoyed in their native land. To obviate these difficulties was the object of the half-way covenant. It provided that all persons of sober life and correct sentiments, without being examined as to a change of heart, might profess religion, or become members of the church, and have their children baptized, though they did not come to

13*

the Lord's table.   The plan originated in Connecticut.   It was formally discussed and adopted at a
meeting of ministers in Boston, in 1657, and ratified
anew in all its essential features, by a general synod
in 1662.*

This mischievous measure, however, was from the
first strongly opposed by many of the most eminent
ministers in the country, and by a still larger number
of the churches; and in this state it was not adopted by a single church till 1696.   But it afterwards
prevailed extensively throughout New-England; and
wherever it did prevail, the consequences were eminently unhappy.   Great numbers came forward to
own the covenant, as it was called, and had their
children baptized; but very few joined the church
in full communion, or partook of the sacrament.   Sat-
isfied with being half-way in the church, and enjoying
a part of its privileges, they settled down in a state of
dull and heartless formality; and felt little or no concern respecting their present condition or future
prospects.   They had found a place, within the pale
of the visible church, which, while it relieved them
from the necessity of repentance and a life of holy
obedience, quieted them in their sins, and gave them

* Trumbull's History of Connecticut, vol. I. 298—310.   Hist.
of Dissenters, vol. II. p. 441.

a comfortable, but deceitful hope of heaven. By receiving into covenant connection such numbers of unsanctified persons, the moral energy of the churches was destroyed ; their distinctive character, as holy communities, was swept away ; the discipline of the gospel could no longer be maintained ; nor the doctrines nor the duties of the gospel be preached and enforced with that clearness and directness which are requisite to give them effect on the heart and life.

This state of things prepared the way for another step in the progress of decline. About the year 1700, Mr. Stoddard, a distinguished minister of Northampton, inferred, with apparent justness, that those, who in virtue of their covenant connexion with the church, had a right to receive baptism for their children, had an equal right to the Lord's supper. This led him on to another conclusion, that the Lord's Supper is among the appointed means of regeneration ; *a converting ordinance ;*——that all persons ought to come to this ordinance, for the same reason, that they ought to attend public worship, or read the Bible ; and consequently, that a profession of piety is not to be required as a qualification for communion in the church.

This doctrine, like the half-way covenant, was at first far from being generally approved either by the ministers or churches. It was regarded as a dangerous innovation, and as directly opposed to the principles and practice of almost all the churches in New England. The matter was publicly controverted between Mr. Stoddard and Dr. Increase Mather of Boston. But "owing to Mr. Stoddard's great influence over the people of Northampton, it was introduced there ; and by degrees it spread very much among ministers and people in that county, and in other parts of New-England."*

The great principle, adopted by the pilgrims in the organization of their churches, and by which alone their purity could be preserved, was now gone. Piety was no longer regarded as an essential qualification for membership in the church. Unconverted persons, those who knew themselves to be such, were received as members of the spiritual body of Christ, and admitted, without examination or restraint, to the special, sealing ordinances of the gospel. This practice 'brought in the first great apostacy of the christian church ;' and wherever it was adopted in New-England, the influence was deplorable. The churches in which it

* Edwards' Works, vol. I. 65.

prevailed, ceased to be, even in profession, societies of sanctified persons; and composed of a strange mixture of the holy with the unholy, they soon lost their vital energies, and sunk into a state of great formality and coldness.

The churches having thus become secularized in their spiritual character, it could not be expected that the ministry would entirely escape the infection. Ministers who were truly pious, could not fail to experience the chilling influence of the coldness and apathy that prevailed around them, and would be greatly straitened and embarassed in the ministration of the word and ordinances of God.   But more than this; many would be likely to enter the ministry who had never experienced the grace of God in their hearts.   And that this, in numerous cases, was the fact, especially during the period that elapsed from 1680 to 1740–50, there is most painful evidence to believe.   The ministers referred to were for the most part, 'grave men; in speculation orthodox, or moderately so, and went the customary round of ministerial duties with a good degree of regularity; but their preaching lacked point, and earnestness, and application; their devotional services lacked warmth and spirituality; their labors were not blessed of the Holy Spirit; their people slum bered, and they slumbered with them, and an aspect of moral desolation and death was spread over the congregations and churches where they labored.'*

As another cause of decline, I venture to mention the custom of supporting religion by law. The ministers of New-England were at first supported by voluntary contributions, usually made at the close of public service on the Sabbath. But this method being found inconvenient and defective, a law was early passed, requiring all to pay for the support of the gospel in proportion to their property. This law, with some modifications, continued in force for more than a hundred and fifty years; and while the country was thinly settled, and the people were nearly all of the same denomination, the law, it cannot be doubted, was productive of much good. It secured to the community a much greater amount of religious instruction, than could have been expected from mere voluntary associations for the support of the gospel. But that the good was counterbalanced by no small amount of evil, cannot, I think, be reasonably questioned. The law, especially in its earliest provisions, did in fact create a religious establishment. It recognized the Congregational churches as the established churches of the

* Spirit of the Pilgrims, 1829: p. 70.

state, and secured to them the special patronage and support of the civil power. What then should prevent the churches of New-England from experiencing, at least in some measure, the disastrous effects, which have always resulted from ecclesiastical establishments? If any thing can be known, with certainty, from the history of such establishments, it is that they invariably tend to beget a spirit of formality and worldliness; to turn off the hopes of ministers and churches from the living God, and to inspire in them a deceptive confidence in an arm of flesh. And this, beyond doubt, was, to some extent, the effect on the ministers and churches of New-England. They lay recumbent on the civil arm, and slumbered in a deceitful security, derived from the protection and support of law. They did not feel their dependance on God, as they would in other circumstances; nor pray nor act with that humility and decision in promoting the cause of religion, which they would have had under a due impression of the great truth, *that salvation is only of the Lord.* Nor is this all. As other denominations multiplied in the community, they complained bitterly of the preference which was supposed to be given to the Congregational churches. Though permitted to worship God in their own way, they were continually inveighing against our churches as the standing order; and early began to exercise that spirit of proselytism, and to cherish those deep rooted prejudices, and to vent those revilings of a hireling priesthood, and those complaints of persecution and oppression, which have not wholly ceased to this day. These causes have not been without their influence. In many cases, they have weakened, and in some, have laid waste the churches in our connection; and to a great extent, they have operated to excite and keep alive prejudice and enmity against the doctrines and order of the Congregational churches.

Besides the causes now specified, others more remote might be mentioned. The bloody wars, which for many years, the colonists were obliged to carry on with the Indians had an unhappy influence upon the interests of religion, and tended to drive from the churches the mild and merciful spirit of the gospel. The wide extension of the new settlements, by which the people were often deprived of the advantages of christian communion and worship, tended to the same result. In many cases, also, there was a rapid increase of property, which kindled pride, and fed covetousness and turned away the hearts of the people from the love and service of God.

But these causes of decline were slight and limited in their operation, compared with the French war, and the war of the Revolution. The first of these wars commenced in 1775, and lasted till 1763. During that period the country was constantly alarmed and agitated, and burdened with taxes, and often plunged in distress and mourning. The public mind was absorbed in other concerns than those of religion ; the tone of christian feeling and sentiment was relaxed, and the cause of Christ greatly neglected.

In the mean time, a multitude of foreigners, officers and soldiers, were spread over the land. Many of these were men of corrupt principles and corrupt morals ; and they were assiduous in their attempts to infuse the poison of their sentiments and practices into the minds of their American associates. And in these attempts they were but too successful. Multitudes of young men and others, drawn away from the quiet pursuits and regular habits of home, to mingle with British soldiers and British officers in the temptations of the field and the camp, soon discovered that they were no dull proficients in the school of infidelity and vice. When they returned home, they had drunk too deeply of the cup, to exchange their new principles and practices, for the sober

14

doctrines and lives of their countrymen. The means which had been pursued to corrupt them, they now pursued to corrupt others; and in this way, the morals and the habits of New England received a shock, the effects of which are felt to the present day.*

Next followed the revolutionary war, which was productive of still more disastrous effects in corrupting the morals and defacing the religious character of New England. The public mind was more deeply excited. The war was carried on in the midst of the people, and all classes, in one way or another, were engaged in it. The consequences were every where felt, and every where visible. The minds of men were drawn away from the great concern of life; their moral sense was blunted; their respect for the law, the truth, and the institutions of God was diminished; and multitudes initiated in the infidel philosophy of France, which now began to spread in the country, threw off the restraints of christian principles as childish, and learned to treat all religion with scorn, as a mere dream of dotards and fit only for children and nurses.

Such to a great extent was the state of public feeling and sentiment at the close of the war; and for

* Dwight's Travels, vol. 4, p. 366.

several years after, it was rather deteriorated than improved. There was no longer that reverence for God, nor that veneration for the Sabbath, nor that regard for truth and justice, nor that unhesitating belief in divine revelation and the great doctrines of the Bible, which were so conspicuous in the character of the first settlers of New England. The principles and characters of its inhabitants were essentially changed ; infidelity and scepticism had already taken deep root, and there was a melancholy preparation for the rapid and extensive spread of error through the country.

I must now notice an event, which, while it is to be regarded as the great cause of restoring moral vigor and purity to the churches of New England, is also to be considered as the *occasion* of introducing many of the errors which have since overspread the land. I refer to the revivals of religion which took place near the middle of the last century. The state of religion was at that time lamentably low. Owing to the influence of the half way covenant and the practice of admitting to the communion those who gave no evidence, and made no profession of piety, the life and power of religion had well nigh departed from the churches, and to a melancholy extent, they were composed of unsanctified members. The ministers were much in the same state. They had not yet renounced the creed of their fathers. They were in the main, orthodox in sentiment and sober in life, but greatly deficient in the spirit and power of the ministry. Their fault was not so much that they preached *error*, as that they did not preach the *truth ;* at least not with that discrimination and force, which were necessary to give it effect in the conversion and moral improvement of men. Their sermons were too generally in the form of dull moral essays, exceedingly defective in evangelical sentiment, in application and point ; and tended rather to build up men in their self righteousness, than to convince them of sin and bring them to Christ for salvation. In short, their existed, extensively, at this time, both in ministers and churches a laxer system of doctrine and practice than had before prevailed in New-England. Hence, President Edwards remarks : "About this time, began the great noise, that was made in this part of the country, about Arminianism, which seemed to appear with a very threatening aspect upon the interests of religion. The friends of vital piety trembled for fear of the issue.*

Such was the state of things, when, in 1734, it pleased God to pour out his spirit in a very wondeful manner. The work commenced in Northampton, under the clear and powerful preaching of Edwards.

* Works, vol. 3, p. 13.

It soon extended into the adjacent region; and many towns in Connecticut were visited. It began in Boston, in 1740, and in that, and the three following years, prevailed to a greater or less degree, in more than one hundred and fifty congregations in New England, and some of the middle and southern states.* In its commencement, the revival was peculiarly still, solemn and powerful; and its fruits eminently holy and precious. But in its progress, many things were connected with it, which were of a very unhappy character, and tended greatly to bring reproach upon the work, and to put a stop to its advancement. There was much intemperate zeal, and extravagance and enthusiasm. Nor is this at all wonderful, when we consider what was the state of the churches and of the ministry. But conceding all that can be claimed with any show of justice, even by the enemies of the revival; there is evidence enough to satisfy every candid, christian mind, that it was indeed what it was declared to be, by the united public testimony of one hundred and sixty ministers, 'a great and precious work of God.' Multitudes were gathered into the fold of Christ, and continued to adorn the doctrine of God their Savior, till by death they were removed to a better world. New life and power

* Dwight's Life of Edwards, p. 191—2.

14*

were breathed into the ministry—a higher and more decided tone of piety was imparted to the churches, and a change effected in the state of religious sentiment and practice, the blessed effects of which remain to the present day.

But as might have been expected, this work of God met with great opposition. It broke the slumbers of the impenitent and prayerless. It reached the consciences of those ministers and members of churches, who were either destitute of piety or were too deeply sunk in moral insensibility to welcome the visitations of the Holy Spirit. They felt themselves reproved and condemned by what they witnessed and heard, and were roused to great hostility and resistance. Many of the ministers preached and wrote against the revival as a work of delusion and fanaticism.* Many of the churches united to resist its progress, and to vilify and reproach all who were in any way engaged in promoting it. The result was, that a large number, both of ministers and churches, took a *permanent* and *decided* stand against revivals of religion, and against those doctrines which

---

* It is not intended to intimate that all, who opposed the revival, were of course destitute of religion. Some real christians were, no doubt, early prejudiced against it, by the false reports of its enemies, and the exceptionable conduct of not a few of its professed friends.

God is wont to bless in producing revivals. For this they were prepared by the previous state of their hearts. They were predisposed to embrace loose Arminian sentiments; and the revival was the occasion of bringing out the feelings of their hearts, and leading them to embrace the errors to which they were before inclined. Here is to be traced the first open departure from the faith of the pilgrims—the first visible, decided step in the progress of that system of error which has since spread its blighting influence over so many of the churches of New-England. Its first form was Arminianism; then followed Pelagianism—then Arianism; and last of all, Socinianism.*

* Very similar to this has been the progress of declension in those churches in England that have renounced the faith of the Nonconformists, and become Unitarian. Among all the dissenting ministers who officiated in London in 1730, there was not one acknowledged Arian, though there were a considerable number who were Arminians. But within thirty years after this, " Arianism spread far and wide in the country, especially in the Presbyterian congregations, both ministers and people." Socinianism, which has been well called the "second stage of the disease," soon supervened, and with very few exceptions has spread itself into all those congregations that had first taken the infection of Arianism. Says an intelligent traveller, " The form which Unitarianism assumes here, [Birmingham] and with very few exceptions throughout the country, is Humanitarianism; insomuch that an Arian congregation,—one of the very few remaining ones in England,—not long since wishing to obtain a minister of their own sentiments, found it a matter of great difficulty; and whether they succeeded at last, I am not quite certain." Dr. Sprague's Letters from Europe. See Hist. of Dissenters, vol. 3, p. 314–328.

Having thus traced some of the principal causes of the decline of religion in New-England, let us next endeavor to mark its extent.

The declension in respect to the spirit of piety commenced at an early period; and it was often deeply deplored by the aged and more experienced ministers.*

*In a sermon preached 1740, by the Rev. Mr. Prince, of the Old South Church, Boston, it is said—"Thus this wonderful work of the grace of God, begun in England and brought over hither, was carried on while the greater part of the first generation lived, for about thirty years; and then the second generation rising up and growing thick upon the stage, a little after 1660, there began to appear a decay: and this increased to 1670, when it grew very visible and threatening, and was generally complained of and bewailed bitterly by the pious among them: and yet much more to 1680, when but few of the first generation remained." So affecting were the evidences of a declining state of religion at this time, that at the instance of the ministers, the Massachusetts government called a synod of the churches in that colony, to consider among other things, these two important questions:—1. What are the evils that have provoked the Lord to bring his judgments on New-England?—2. What is to be done, that so these evils may be reformed? By the recommendation of the synod, many of the churches solemnly renewed their covenant with God and one another; the consequences of which were eminently happy. Says Cotton Mather, " Verily remarkable was the blessing of God on the churches that did not so sleep, as some others; not only by a great advancement of holiness in the people, but also by a great addition of converts to their holy fellowship. Many thousand spectators will testify that they never saw the special presence of the great God our Savior more notably discovered than in the solemnity of these opportunities." Christian Hist. vol. I. p. 94—98—107.

In 1668 a venerable minister, in a sermon preached before the Legislature of Massachusetts, says, " Alas how is New England in danger, this day, to be lost, even in New England ; to be buried in its own ruins ?   How sadly may we lament it, that all are not Israel that are now of Israel ? How is the good grain diminished, and the chaff increased ?   The first generation have been reproved, time after time, and the most of them gathered in as shocks of corn in their season ; but we who rise up to tread the foot-steps of those 'that have gone before us, alas ! what are we !   What coolings and abatements are there charged upon us, in the things that are good, and that have been our glory ?   We have abated in our esteem of ordinances, in our hungering and thirsting after the rich provisons of the house of God.   We have abated in our love and zeal, in our wise, tender and faithful management of that great duty of mutual watchfulness and reproof."*

In 1702, Dr. Increase Mather, in a work entitled, the Glory departing from New England, says, " Look into pulpits, and see if there is such a glory there as once there was.   New England has had teachers, eminent for learning and no less eminent for holiness and all ministerial accomplishments.   When will

* Mr. Stoughton's Election Sermon.

Boston see a Cotton, and a Norton again? When will New England see a Hooker, a Shepard, a Mitchell, not to mention others? There are ministers who are not like their predecessors, nor principled, nor spirited as they were. No little part of the glory was laid in the dust when these eminent servants of Christ were laid in their graves. Look into our civil state; does Christ reign there as once he did? How many churches, how many towns are there in New England, that we may sigh over them and say, *The glory is gone!*" O, if this venerable servant of God saw such cause for lamentation and mourning in his day, what would be his emotions were he to visit the scene of his labors and look round upon the churches, where once he preached and prayed and ministered the bread of life? Truly may it be said of those churches, *the glory is gone.* And the same lamentation may be uttered over many other churches of New-England. There is a melancholy decay of piety visible throughout this land of our pilgrim fathers. There is no longer that reverence for God, and regard for his institutions; no longer that purity of morals and general correctness of sentiment, nor that disinterestedness and zeal for the public good which " dignified and adorned the age of New-England's simplicity." The evidences of our degeneracy will appear in the following particulars:

1. In an extensive disregard and neglect of religious institutions. These, by our pious ancestors, were held in the highest estimation. For the enjoyment of them, they were willing to forego any worldly good, or to make any worldly sacrifices; and that their posterity might prize and enjoy them in all future generations, was the object of their daily prayers and deepest solicitude.

But by how many of their descendants, are the institutions of the gospel utterly neglected and despised? How many towns and parishes are there in New-England, that are waste places, on which no rain or dew of heaven descends, and where no sound of spiritual life and mercy is ever heard? What numbers are scattered over this land of the pilgrims, who rarely, if ever, hear a christian sermon, or enter a place of christian worship, and who prefer their covetousness to the blessings of the gospel, and regard every dollar that is given for the support of the gospel, as no better than lost? O what an affecting sight would it be to our fathers, to behold such multitudes of their posterity, in this very land which they planted with churches and Bibles and the means of salvation, living without hope and without God in the world, selling their birthright as a thing of naught, and turning their back upon all the institutions and blessings of the glorious gospel ?

In the early days of New-England, the Sabbath was esteemed a delight, the holy of the Lord, honorable. Its sanctity was guarded by efficient laws, and all classes of men, legislators, magistrates, and heads of families, were zealously engaged to secure, by the whole weight of their authority and example, a due observance of that holy day.

But the profanation of the Sabbath has now become so common, that it has almost ceased to be regarded as a sin. The laws protecting its sacredness, have long since been swept away, or sleep as a dead letter in the statute book,—attesting thus, both the piety of our ancestors, and the degeneracy of their descendants.

The duty of maintaining family religion, was once universally acknowledged in New-England, and seriously practised in nearly all the families in the land. Every day, the scriptures were read and God worshipped ; and not a child or a servant was suffered to grow up, without being instructed in the principles of religion, and taught to reverence the day, the word and the name of God.

But how sad a contrast is now exhibited ? How

many thousands of families there are in which no prayer is heard, and no thanks rendered, and no worship in any form offered to the great Father of mercies and Giver of all good?   It would seem as if many parents never had a thought respecting the spiritual and immortal interests of their children; but as if their existence and their happiness were confined wholly to this life, and they had nothing either to hope or to fear in the life to come, they appear anxious only to train them up for the pleasures and enjoyments of the present world.   O how melancholy a departure is this from the early habits of New-England? and how dismal the effects which result from it, in the multiplication of prayerless families and prayerless persons ?   O if God should now execute the sentence, *pour out thy fury upon the families that call not on thy name*, how would the smoke of the land ascend up like the smoke of Sodom, and lamentation and wo be heard in every part of it ?

For a long time after the settlement of the country, New-England was eminently distinguished for the purity and strictness of its morals.   Lying and deception, oppression and fraud, intemperance and profaneness, and other kindred vices, were comparatively unknown in the land, and were regarded, universally, with abhorrence.   But now, how aw-

15

fully common ?   How often is the glorious name of
Jehovah profaned in our streets ? How extensive
and terrible is the brutal sin of intemperance ? How
widely extended too is the dreadful sin of falsehood,
in the various forms of evasion, duplicity and hollow
hearted profession ; of lying, and perjury, and breach
of trust, and violation of oaths of office ?   The times
in which we live, are strongly marked with a spirit
of deception and double dealing ; of artful accom-
modation and deceitful management.   Men are every where seen putting on masks, and walking in dis-
guise.   They speak with flattering lips and a double
tongue ; say one thing and mean another.   They
have no principle, no integrity—all is insincere and
hollow-hearted.   They have no frankness, no open-
ness—all is cunning and concealment—all is duplicity and management.   How lamentably visible is all
this, not only in the humble, but the higher walks of
life ; not only in private, but in public stations ; not
only in the petty town or parish meeting, but in the
grand council of the nation !   Time was, when in
New-England, the freeman's oath meant something ;
when the electoral franchise was deemed a sacred
trust ; and when in the exercise of it men felt themselves bound to regard God and conscience and the
good of the community.   But how lamentable a

change has taken place in these respects! How wide and general a departure is there, in the exercise of civil rights and in the performance of civil duties, from the true spirit and intent of our institutions—from all that is free, unbiassed and equitable—from the solemn obligations assumed in the oaths of those who elect, and of those who are elected! What eagerness for office,—how unfaithful to perform the duties of office! What indeed, in a multitude of cases, are oaths of office worth? Nothing. The men who take them are frequently the first to violate the very laws which they had solemnly sworn to maintain and execute. Conscience, integrity, the honor of God and the public good,—what are they in competition with ambition, with self-interest and party spirit? A dust in the balance. By multitudes they are sacrificed without a thought of guilt or a feeling of remorse; and the frequency and impunity with which this is done, argues a deep apostacy from the principles and habits which characterized the people of New-England in the days of her primitive glory.

To our pious ancestors, the doctrines of grace were exceedingly precious. Their excellent characters were formed under the influence of these doctrines. They were the main-spring of their en-

terprize, their zeal, their self-denial and devotedness
to the service of God and the good of mankind.   In
the belief and defence of them, they bid adieu to
their native land ; encountered the perils of the
ocean ; became exiles, and labored, and prayed, and
died in this wilderness, that the doctrines they held
so precious might become the light and the salvation
of their descendants in all future time.

But how many are there in this land of the pilgrims, who now oppose and reject these doctrines,
as ' austere and gloomy,' as ' irrational and absurd,'
as ' chilling to the affections and debasing to the
mind ?' How many substitute, for the holy, humbling,
sanctifying truths held by our fathers, a system which
flatters men in their sins, and feeds their self-right-
eousness and false hopes,—a system, which leaves
the conscience undisturbed, and the heart unimpres-
sed, and ministers quietness and ease to impenitence
and unbelief,—a system, which satisfies and soothes
the gay and the worldly in a course of self-indulgence
and estrangement from God ; which ' mocks at the
seriousness, and spirituality, and self-devotion of true
religion, and considers all the tenderness of an awak-
ened conscience and anxiety for the salvation of the
soul, all the solemnities of conviction of sin, as well
as all joy and peace in believing, the object of ridicule
and sarcasm ?'

The fathers of New-England believed in the divinity of our Lord Jesus Christ ; and were accustomed to honor him, even as they honored the Father. But the advocates of the system alluded to, at least the greater part of them, believe Christ to be a mere man ;* and that to pay him religious homage, would be idolatry.†

* Prof. Stuart, in his Letters to Dr. Channing, says,* " A short time since, almost all the Unitarians in New England, were simple Arians.   Now, there are scarcely any of the younger preachers who have not become simple Humanitarians."   This was in 1819.

In an article published in the Christian Register, August 1826, the editor says,—" *Some* at least among the Unitarians still hold that tenet," (the pre-existence of Christ,) admitting of course that only a few hold it.

The number of Arians in the Unitarian connection has every year been diminishing, and that of Humanitarians increasing. The young men who have come out as ministers of late years among them are nearly all Humanitarians.   This is spoken advisedly.   Those who are best acquainted with facts will be the last to call in question its correctness.   The truth is, the whole tendency of the system is downward.   The account given by Dr. Priestly of the progress of his own mind on this subject is an exact history of the course pursued by hundreds and thousands who have embraced Unitarianism.   He says : " He was once a Calvinist, and that of the strictest sect ; then a high Arian, next a low Arian ; then a Socinian ; in a little time a Socinian of the lowest kind, in which Jesus Christ is considered a mere man, as fallible and peccable as Moses, or any other prophet.   He adds, *I do not know when my creed will be fixed.*

† That to pay religious worship to Christ is considered by Unitarians idolatry, it would be easy to show from their writings; and on their principles no conclusion is more just.

* p. 175.

15*

Our fathers believed that Christ gave himself a *ransom* for sinners ; that *he died, a propitiatory sacrifice, that he might redeem us unto God by his blood.* But now we are told, that he died simply as a martyr in the cause of truth ; that the only effect of his sufferings and death, is to give efficacy to his instructions in reforming the lives of men, and thus qualifying them for forgiveness ; that the doctrine of atonement, as held by the Orthodox, ' is dishonorable to God,' that it ' calumniates his character' and ' throws gloom over the universe ;' and by some, it is openly declared, that they would ' resort to the less chilling creed of the atheist, rather than admit it.'*

Our fathers believed that man is a fallen, depraved being, destitute of holiness, and that before he can do works pleasing in the sight of God, he must be regenerated or born of the Spirit.   But the system

In a conversation on some of the fundamental doctrines of religion, Dr. Priestly once said to Professor Miller of Princeton : " I do not wonder that you Calvinists entertain and express a strongly unfavorable opinion of us Unitarians.   The truth is, there neither *can,* nor *ought to be,* any compromise between us.   If you are right, we are not christians at all ; and if we are right, you are *gross idolaters.*

See Dr. Miller's Sermon at the ordination of Rev. Mr. Nevins, Baltimore.

* See Dr. Channing's Dedication Sermon at New-York, 1826, and Rev. Mr. Lamson's Ordination Sermon at Danvers.

which is now becoming fashionable in New-England, rejects this doctrine as false, and injurious to the character of God ; insisting that 'man is by nature no more inclined or disposed to vice than to virtue,' and that ' wickedness, so far from being the prevailing part of human character, makes but an inconsiderable part of it ;'* and as to regeneration, they describe it as a change, either from the Jewish religion, or the idolatrous religion of the gentiles, to an open profession and sincere belief of the christian religion ; but that the term " is without meaning, when applied to those who have been born and educated under the gospel."†

By our pious ancestors justification by faith, through the atonement and mediation of Christ, was esteemed a doctrine of the greatest importance ; and on it, living and dying, they hung all their hopes of pardon and acceptance with God. But by the advocates of what is called liberal christianity, this doctrine is rejected. They say that ' to build the hope of pardon on the independent and infinite sufficiency of Jesus Christ, is to build on an unscriptural and false foundation." " Those persons deceive themselves, who in the apprehension of death, lay hold on

* Dr. Ware's Letters to Trin. and Calv. p. 24.
† Chris. Disciple, 1822, p. 419, 420.

the merits of Christ, and expect to enter heaven in consequence."*

It was once the faith of New-England, that the present life is the only period of probation ; that all who die in their sins are forever lost ; and that according to the Bible, the wicked will, at the last day, *come forth unto the resurrection of damnation*, and *go away into everlasting punishment*. But on this subject of amazing interest, the system now in view, has long since symbolized with Universalism, and now, with perhaps some exceptions, goes hand in hand with the abettors of that false and delusive doctrine.† It likewise rejects the existence of fallen angels, representing the language of scripture on this subject, as 'imagery, borrowed from oriental philosophy, and not to be taken in a literal sense.' The term satan, is only a 'personification of the principle of evil.'‡

---

* Chris. Disciple, New Series, vol. 1, p. 440.

† If it be said that many Unitarians believe in a future state of retribution, the same is true of many Universalists. "The doctrine of a limited future punishment, says the author of the Modern History of Universalism, (p. 434) has never excited a very general interest among Universalists. For twenty years a difference of opinion has existed on this point ; but the difference has not been the cause of alienation of feeling, or disruption of fellowship." For proof of the fact asserted in the text, see Spirit of the Pilgrims, Apr. 1830. Also, Dr Bancroft's Sermons, p. 391–409.

‡ Improved version of the New-Testament, passim ; Letters of Canonicus to Dr. Channing, and Ware's Sermons.

Our ancestors fully believed the Bible to be the word of God. They believed, with the Apostle, *that all scripture is given by inspiration of God, and that in composing the sacred volume, holy men of God spake as they were moved by the Holy Ghost.* But this cardinal, fundamental truth is now rejected, and the doctrine is proclaimed, both from the pulpit and the press, that the ' Scriptures are not a revelation, but only the *record* of a revelation,'*——that ' the compo-

* The meaning of this language seems to be something like this : Christ was a messenger sent from God to make known his will to mankind. What he taught, therefore, was by inspiration, and is to be received as of divine authority. But tho Evangelists, who wrote the New Testament, were not inspired. In recording what Christ taught and did, they simply wrote as honest well meaning men, liable of course like other men to make mistakes, and to adopt ' false and inconclusive reasoning.' The history therefore, which they have given us of the life and teachings of Christ, is to be regarded as a work of their own unaided powers ; as " possessing a properly and purely human character." Hence Unitarians make a wide distinction between the gospels and the epistles. The former, containing an account of what *Christ* taught, are regarded as of higher authority than the latter, which contain only the opinions and reasonings of uninspired men.—— The reason for making this distinction is obvious. " I never knew a man," says Orton, " make a distinction between the gospels and epistles, but the reason was apparent. He was a Socinian ; and finding little about the sacrifice and atonement of Christ in the evangelists, (as there could not be much before our Lord's death) and finding the doctrine run through every page of all the epistles, he was willing to sink the character of the epistles, and lessen men's ideas of them, in order to support his favorite notions."— Letters to Dissenting Ministers, vol. I. p. 136–7.

sition of the Bible is a human work'—a work produced by the natural operation of human thought and feeling; that the Scriptures, so far as their composition is concerned, are to be regarded as possessing a properly and purely human character; the language, comparisons and arguments used in them to enforce the communication being altogether a human work.*

It is asserted moreover, that 'if a philosopher of a mind as enlarged as that of Cicero, and of as high and pure moral sentiments, had lived in the apostolic age, believed Christ to be a messenger from God, and had carefully committed to writing what information he could then obtain concerning his character, miracles and doctrines, subjoining his own explanations and remarks, such a work would have been at least of equal value with any book which remains to us of the New Testament.'†

The fathers of New-England believed in the special influences of the Holy Spirit, and in conversion and revivals of religion as the effect of such influences; and many were the seasons in which magistrates

---

* Christian Examiner, for Jan. 1830.   With this representation let the reader compare 2 Pet. i. 21.   2 Tim. iii. 16.   Gal. i. 11. 1 Cor. ii. 13.

† Christian Examiner, for July, 1829.

and ministers and people united in praying for this richest of heaven's blessings on themselves, on their children, and the community at large ; and when the blessing was enjoyed, they poured out their hearts in devout thanksgivings to God for the bestowment of it.   But now the special influences of the Spirit are discarded as a delusion, and revivals of religion are reproached as the reveries of fanatics ; and even ministers publicly deride and preach against them, as the work of enthusiasm and priestcraft, and altogether of pernicious tendency.

Our fathers considered the church of Christ a community distinct from the world.   They believed that every church ought to consist only of those who have been renewed by the Spirit of God, " sanctified in Christ Jesus, called to be saints ;" and most carefully did they guard the purity of their churches by requiring of all whom they received to their communion, evidence of personal piety and a public profession of their faith in the great doctrines of the gospel.

But now the idea of a church as distinct from the congregation is openly denied.   It is affirmed that ' the distinction attempted to be kept up between the two, is in most respects artificial and without a counterpart in nature ;' that the sacrament of the

Lord's supper 'should be open alike to all ;' and that we have no more business to shut up this ordinance to a peculiar and chosen few, than we have to treat in a similar manner any of the public services of the sanctuary. It is said moreover, that 'no examination of candidates for ordination, or for admission to our communion or fellowship, with whatever softening pretence it may be proposed, should ever be acquiesced in.'* To crown all, the men of this system assure us, that mere error is innocent and of no account. 'The denunciations of heaven,' it is said, 'were never uttered against error of faith, but error of practice.' 'Jesus neither condemned, censured nor judged any man for his errors.'† And yet with marvellous consistency they denounce the whole system of the orthodox 'as absurd, unscriptural and pernicious ;' that they consider transubstantiation itself a less monstrous doctrine than the five points of Calvin.‡

Such are some of the characteristics of the system which now prevails in some parts of New-England ; and such the marks which indicate the nature and extent of our apostacy from the faith and piety

* Christian Disciple, 1822, p. 54.
† Unit. Mis. 1822, p. 175, and 1821, p. 54.
‡ Chris. Examiner, vol. III. p. 76.

of our fathers. The defection commenced about seventy or eighty years ago; and the first visible form which it assumed was Arminianism. It soon passed through the intermediate changes of Pelagianism and Arianism; and having in the latter form, *chiefly by concealment*,* worked its way into some of the pulpits and infected some of the churches of the metropolis of Massachusetts and its immediate vicinity, it broke out about fifteen years ago in the form of Socinianism. The system is still most evidently on the descending scale;† and where it will stop, it would be unseasonable to predict. It has long been tending to a single point; and that is, whether the Bible is an inspired book, and its decisions final and authoritative in matters of faith. That point it has already reached in Germany, and many parts of Great Britain;‡ and though in our own country,

* For evidence of this fact, see Spirit of the Pilgrims, Mar. 1830.

† See Hist. of American Unitarianism, and the Review of this work, in the Panoplist for June, 1815.

‡ The ablest critics among the Liberalists in Germany, do not hesitate to admit that the leading doctrines of the orthodox system are taught in the New-Testament. But then the authority of Paul, and John, and Peter is not decisive with this class of Theologians.* They claim the same right to examine and try *their* sentiments, at the bar of human reason, that they do the sentiments of other men.

* See Stuart's Letters, second edit. p. 167.

16

there are many advocates of the system, who seem
reluctant to approach this point, and start back as
they look over and see the gulf beneath, still not a
few are boldly treading towards it, and only wait a
favorable opportunity,—the rising up of some able
intrepid leader,—to step forward and openly avow
the principle that the Bible is not decisive authority
in questions of faith.

Descendants of New-England!—Sons and Daughters of the pilgrims!—forsake not the God of your
fathers; turn not away from that religion, in the
light of which they sojourned on earth, and in the
comforts and hopes of which, they ascended to
glory!—forget not the character of your fathers,
nor lightly throw away the institutions and principles
and hopes which they have bequeathed to you, as a
rich legacy from Heaven!—renounce not your pa-
rentage—renounce not your Bibles, nor your hopes
of salvation; nor throw yourselves within the influ-

In 1819, Professor Stuart, in his Letters to Dr. Channing, ven-
tured to predict that the ' lapse of a few years would bring the
Unitarians, in this country, to an undisguised avowal of German
divinity, in all its latitude ;' and that the question between them
and the orthodox would soon be, " whether natural or revealed
religion is our guide and our hope."*   The rapid progress, since
made towards the fulfilment of this prediction, has exceeded all
that was then anticipated, and leaves little room to doubt as to
the final result.

* pp. 171–175.

ence of that delusive system which is sweeping so fast into those regions of error, where the Spirit of God never comes, and the voice of redeeming mercy is never heard !

And now in conclusion, who of us can refrain from lifting up his heart to God in devout thanksgiving, that amidst all the apostacies and errors and sins which have swept over the land of the pilgrims, he has still a seed to serve him—I will not say a faithful few, but a faithful many ?   The evangelical Congregational churches of New England were never in a more prosperous state than at present. They never included so large a number of pious, devoted members ; they were never blessed with a more intelligent and faithful ministry ; they were never more united in sentiment and never cheered by brighter prospects.   The banner of the pilgrims still waves over the land, and on it is still borne the animating inscription, *Qui translulit sustinet.*   Let us pray that it may remain there forever ; and that all posterity may experience the fulfilment of its significant meaning—*He that brought us over will still sustain us.*   Yes, blessed be God, the vine which he brought out of Egypt and planted here, still lives and flourishes.   Yes, though many have been engaged to break down its hedges—though the boar out of the wood

has often threatened to waste it, and the wild beast
of the field to devour it, it still lives and flourishes;
it has struck deep its roots, and its boughs are like
the goodly cedars.——It has shot forth more than a
thousand branches in its native soil, and its boughs
extend to the far distant parts of the land.   Let it
still flourish; its leaves are for the healing of the nations, and blessed are all they that repose under the
shadow thereof.

LECTURE VI.

MEANS OF RECOVERY AND DEFENCE.

JEREMIAH vi. 16.

THUS SAITH THE LORD, STAND YE IN THE WAYS AND SEE, AND ASK FOR THE OLD PATHS, WHERE IS THE GOOD WAY, AND WALK THEREIN, AND YE SHALL FIND REST FOR YOUR SOULS.

THIS scripture, with which I commenced these Lectures I deem as appropriate as any other to close them ; because having stood in the ways and seen, and asked for the old paths and found, as we trust, where is the good way, it seems proper to conclude, with an enforcement of the exhortation, to walk therein, that we may find rest for our souls.

Accordingly it is the object of the present Lecture to consider *the means, and urge the duty of maintaining and defending* the order and principles of the Congregational churches of New England. The announcement of the object implies the existence of danger. And danger does exist. The condition of these churches is no longer what it once was. A great change has taken place in the character and circumstances of the community. Numerous other

16*

denominations have risen up around and in the midst of the churches planted by the Pilgrims; and it is not to be disguised, that many of them look with no friendly eye upon these ancient and venerable watch towers of the gospel. The very position, which our churches, for a long time, held, as the sole occupants of the ground, and which they now hold, as the largest and most influential denomination in New England, excites the sleepless jealousy of minor sects that are opposed to our doctrines and discipline; and facts are not wanting to show, that however divided they are among themselves, they are not backward to unite in carrying on a warfare against what is deemed a common enemy.

At the same time, the very cause, which excites the jealousy, and quickens the spirit of proselytism in other denominations around us, operates to infuse a spirit of inactivity and slumber into our own denomination. *We are in danger from our number and strength.* Confident of the correctness of our principles, and of the stability of the foundation on which they rest, we are liable to cherish a feeling of false security, and to overlook the causes which are, secretly, or more openly, operating to undermine and lay waste our goodly inheritance. For a long period after the settlement of the country, our religious institutions existed and flourished almost without the agency or care of the people attached to them. They were organized by our pious ancestors, and the community, where they were located, continued to enjoy the blessings flowing from them, with scarcely thinking of the source whence they sprung, or of the possibility of that source being cut off or exhausted. We have never, as a denomination, been trained to defend our principles, or guard our rights. We have taken no pains to cultivate or extend a denominational feeling. Rarely has any thing been heard, either from the pulpit or the press, designed to illustrate the grounds of our church order, or to show the excellence of our modes of worship. Devoted to what have been justly considered more important interests, we have hardly given a thought to external forms, or bestowed any labor upon the outward frame work of our churches.

But circumstances have now changed. The means of safety, which were once deemed sufficient, cannot now be relied upon without extreme presumption. The members of our churches and congregations must study and understand the principles of their own order; they must be made acquainted with the peculiar duties which are imposed upon them by the change of the times; and must realize the necessity of wise, decided and persevering exertions to sustain the interests which have come down to us, so precious a heritage from our pilgrim ancestors.

In pointing out the means by which this is to be attempted, our attention is, in the first place, directed to the *christian ministry.* There never was a class of men on whom rested weightier responsibilities, than on the Congregational ministers of New-England. They have entered into the labors of men, honored of God as instruments in establishing his church in this western world. The interests entrusted to them are of immense value ; and at this day, especially, can be maintained only by *great, persevering and well-directed labors.*

The first and great thing demanded of ministers is, a plain and faithful declaration of the whole counsel of God. This is fundamental. It is the grand appointed means of reviving religion when it is decayed; and of keeping alive in the church a spirit of affectionate, fruitful piety. No historical fact is sustained by fuller evidence, than that the great apostacies that have, at different periods, taken place in the church, commenced in a concealment, or partial exhibition of the distinguishing truths of the gospel. The defection began in the ministry, and was extended to the churches, and the people at large, through the medium of a smooth, deceptive style of preaching. This is eminently true of the defection from orthodoxy which has overspread so large a portion of Germany. It is also true of the lamentable apostacy which has taken place in many churches in Great Britain.*

* See in the Spirit of the Pilgrims for Feb. 1830, an article on the state of religion in Germany ; also, Hist. of Dissenters, vol. 3, p. 314.

In a pamphlet published by Bretschneider, a learned German theoligian of the liberal school, the following facts are stated respecting the indifference to religion which prevails in that country where the New Theology, or the doctrine of the Rationalists has taken the deepest root and produced the most fruit. " He states that this indifference is spread among all classes, that the Bible used to be found in every house—that very many made it a law to read a chapter every day, or at least every Sunday ; that it must have been a very poor family, where a Bible was not a part of the marriage portion, but that now very many do not possess one or let it lie neglected in a corner,—that now hardly one fifth of the inhabitants of towns receive the sacrament or confess ; that few attend the churches, which are now too large, though fifty years ago they were too small ; that few honor Sunday, but that many make it a day for private business, or for work, and that there are now few students in theology, compared with those of law and medicine ; and that if things go on thus, there will short- ly not be persons to supply the various ecclesiastical offices. Within sixty years, he says, the sermons have changed very much ; and in contents, tone and form, have followed the spirit of the age, insomuch that many, instead of preaching on the doc- trines of Christianity, betook themselves to the more useful sub- jects of politics and agriculture, &c. This writer does indeed try to prove that the new fancies of the Rationalists had not produced this indifference ; but here Tittman directly contradicts him, and positively testifies that the consequence of the prevalence of their

And it is equally true of the churches in this country, that have renounced the truth, and gone over to the side of heresy. The mischief, in all these cases, commenced in the ministry, and showed itself first in a *cautious, concealed* manner of preaching the *truth.* The ministers, who first adopted this manner, were

sentiments was distrust and suspicion of the doctrines of Christianity, among all classes ; and an entire indifference to religion."

See *Biblical Repertory for Jan.* 1827. *p.* 4—5.

The following facts, respecting the process of decay in many of the Dissenting churches in England, are from Bogue and Bennett's History of Dissenters.

" In many places, *indolence* diffused through the dissenting congregation its benumbing influence. It could not be said that the doctrine of the preacher was contrary to truth. But he did not breathe his soul into his sermons. His words appeared to freeze upon his lips. The people felt the chilling impulse, and on their faces might be read cold insensibility, and frozen indifference."

" But during this period (from 1714 to 1760) *error* was the destroying angel of dissenting congregations. In the ordinary course of things, in proportion as dissenting ministers have departed from those religious principles which were held by the men ejected from the establishment for nonconformity, they have reduced the number of their audience. Whenever they have departed from what is called Calvinism, the congregation has evidently felt the change : it has been arrested in its growth, and, after a time visibly decayed."

" In whatever communions Arminianism may have had crouded places of worship, it never had this effect among dissenters ; but almost without an exception, was the first stage of a congregational decline. Arianism may be called the second stage of the disease, and where it filled the pulpit, invariably emptied the pews. Where Socinianism found an entrance, its operations were quicker than those of the Arian creed and more effectual ; flourishing soci-

not themselves heterodox. They believed the essential doctrines of the gospel, and occasionally preached them; but 'not the whole'—'not in their fulness'—not in their undisguised simplicity and plainness, nor in a close and fearless application of them to the heart and conscience. There was in their dis-

eties were reduced to a few families, which being animated with zeal for the new opinions, or indifferent about any, chose to continue to support the modes of worship, to which from education or use, they were attached. In many places, Socinianism was the abomination of desolation, and consigned what had formerly been the house of prayer and of the assemblies of the saints, an undisturbed abode, to the spiders and the bats."

"But it may be asked, is no exception to be made in favor of congregations in which religion flourished? An Arian congregation, under an Arian minister, whose religion was in a flourishing state, perhaps cannot be named in the whole of England, since the day that James Pierce preached that doctrine within the walls of his new meeting at Exeter."

Describing the state of religion among the Dissenters from the accession of George the third to 1808, the authors say :—"Many who drank the cup of Arianism first, and then of Socinianism to the very dregs, ceased to be members of the dissenting congregation; and with a perfect hatred of the doctrines of the church of England, pusillanimously and disingenuously bore a part in her very explicit Trinitarian worship. By the operation of these causes many a Presbyterian congregation dwindled from a giant into a dwarf. They are in general now but the shadow of what they formerly were, and many of them have ceased to exist. Devonshire, the cradle of Arianism, has been the grave of the Arian dissenters ; and there is not left in that populous county, a twentieth part of the Presbyterians which were to be found at her birth. More than twenty of their meeting houses, it is said have been shut up ; and in those which remain open there are to be

courses a wretched sterility of evangelical sentiment and feeling. They were afraid, perhaps, that a plain and full exhibition of the truth would give offence; and, therefore, kept it back, or presented it in such a *disguised, partial, pointless manner*, as to deprive it entirely of its power to awaken and convince.——

seen the skeletons only of congregations which were full and flourishing before error had banished prosperity."

"In other counties of England where these sentiments prevailed, the effects have been the same. Like the devouring pestilence, Arianism and Socinianism have, with few exceptions, carried desolation with them into every congregation where they have obtained an entrance; and some scores more of their meeting houses would have been shut up but for *the pious benevolence of persons of a different creed in the former generation. By their endowments*, many of the present Presbyterian ministers have been enabled to retain their office, and to preach to what deserves not the name of a congregation, but is better described by the prophets account of what remains after the shaking of the olive tree: two or three berries on the top of the uppermost bough, four or five on the outmost fruitful branches thereof. So great is the change which these sentiments have produced, that perhaps there are not now in England twelve of their congregations which can boast an attendance of five hundred people; whereas before the introduction of Arianism they could in more than two hundred places count five hundred hearers, and in several, more than double that number."

Hist. of Diss. vol. 3, p. 314—vol. 4, p. 120.

The important and very instructive facts disclosed in these extracts are a sufficient apology for the length of them. They deserve to be deeply pondered, as they show the tendency of lax preaching, and especially the fatal influence of Arian and Socinian sentiments wherever they prevail.

Having gone so far, as through fear or favor, to conceal or partially exhibit the great doctrines of the gospel, the next step was to regard these doctrines as of little practical importance—as mere speculative points, and to substitute for them, the preaching of a dull and heartless morality. This prepared the way for the coming in of Arminianism, then of Arianism, and last of all, of Socinianism. The connection is perfectly obvious; and can be traced back directly to a want of decision and plainness on the part of the ministry, in declaring the truths of God's word. It is the most wretched policy that can be adopted, to attempt to build up the cause of God by a compromise of his truth. Its uniform effect is to destroy the life and power of the ministry—to weaken and scatter the congregation, and in the end, to establish the reign of error and sin. God has appointed his own means of building up his kingdom. They are the truths of his gospel, ministered in fidelity, and made efficacious on the heart by the power of the Holy Spirit. And the minister who rejects these means, for others of his own devising; who substitutes policy for duty, and relies on temporizing expedients, instead of the blessing of God on a faithful declaration of his truth, will have the mor-

17

tification to see his wisdom turned into folly, and the curse of heaven resting on all his labors.

Let a timid, time-serving policy then be forever banished from the ministry. It has done more than any other one cause to scatter the seeds of error, and multiply the waste places of our land. It was not by such a policy that our fathers established the churches of New-England; nor is it by such a policy, that they can be sustained and built up, and their moral influence diffused through the community.—— What God requires of the pastors of these churches is, that they stand up fearlessly for his cause and truth, and proclaim, in the fullest and most direct manner, the doctrines of his word, *trusting him for the consequences.* If there are those in our congregations who cannot endure such an exhibition of truth, it is far better they should retire, than that any attempt should be made to retain them, by a concealment or partial delivery of God's message. Every such attempt is wrong in itself; and never fails to weaken the hands and lessen the influence of a minter. The ambassador of Christ always purchases peace at a most dear rate, when he does it by a sacrifice of truth and duty.

It is no time, let me further say, to withhold from the people, the disitnguishing doctrines of

the gospel, or to substitute in their place, vague
and general statements, or a light and flimsy decla-
mation, when, as now, the enemy is coming in
like a flood, and foundations are being shaken and
swept away. Ministers are especially called upon,
at the present day, to dwell upon these doctrines
with much frequency and earnestness ; to preach
them with great clearness and force ; with great
cogency of argument, illustration and appeal.—
Their discourses should be instinct with feeling and
intelligence ; with spirit and power ; appealing directly to the understanding and conscience, and
coming home to the feelings and wants of men. The
spirit of the age does not tolerate a dull, scholastic,
spiritless manner of giving religious instruction ;—
the gospel does not tolerate such a manner. It is a
generous, expansive, noble system of truth, bearing
directly and powerfully on all the relations, duties
and hopes of men ; and when narrowed down, as it
too often is, to a few common-place topics, constantly recurring, and with little or no variety of illustration, it loses its native character and power, and becomes a dry, frigid, lifeless thing. To interest the
minds of men, and produce its proper effect on the
heart and life, it demands to be presented in its own
native glory ; to be unfolded in all its wide relations
and affecting consequences; to be preached, in adap-

tation to the spirit of the times ; with affection and
fervor ; with clearness of thought and closeness of
application and appeal.   And facts abundantly testify, that whenever the gospel is thus preached, it
attracts attentive hearers, gathers flourishing congregations, and builds up the church in holiness and
love.   Notwithstanding all the reproach that is cast
upon the evangelical system of doctrines, one thing
is indisputable—it is of all systems the best adapted
to excite attention and interest feeling ; and the only
system that can be relied upon to preserve a congregation from decay, or to revive it when it is decayed.
So strong a conviction have I of this truth, that I am
fully persuaded, that if the evangelical ministers of
New-England were, but for a short time, to change
their strain of preaching for one more lax and accom-
modating, it would be the ruin of their cause—the
means of vacating their places of worship, and spreading indifference and worldliness and death among all
classes of their hearers.*

* " When you have the opportunity of seeing and observing more
of the state of religion in our congregations, you will find what I
have long since found (and -every year that I live increases my
conviction of it,) that when ministers entertain their people with
lively and pretty things, confine themselves to general har-
rangues, insist principally on moral duties without enforcing them
warmly and affectionately by evangelical motives ; while they
neglect the peculiars of the gospel ; never or seldom display the
grace of God and the love of Christ in our redemption ; the ne-

Let the pastors of our churches, then, realize their responsibility, and resolve, with Paul, to know nothing among their people ‘save Jesus and him crucified.’

cessity of regeneration and sanctification by a constant depend- ance upon the Holy Spirit of God for assistance and strength in the duties of the christian life ; their congregations are in a wretched state ; some are dwindling to nothing, as is the case with several in this neighborhood, where there are not now as many scores as there were hundreds in their meeting places fifty years ago.

But when by trade and manufactures, new persons come to the place and fill up the vacant seats, there is a fatal deadness spread over the congregation. They run in the course of the world, fol- low every fashionable folly ; and family and personal godliness seem in general to be lost among them. There is scarcely any appearance of life and zeal in the cause of religion which de- mands and deserves the greatest.

Whereas, on the contrary, I never knew an instance where a minister was a pious serious man, whose strain was evangelical and affectionate, but his congregation kept up, though death and removals had made many breaches in it. And in general minis- ters of this latter sort have had more affection and respect from their people than the former."

Orton's Letters to Dissenting Ministers, vol. 1, p. 100.

"I see no connection between Calvinistical sentiments and zealous useful labors, but I have long observed with great surprise that our orthordox brethren in the church and among the dissent- ers, are in general most serious and active in their ministry ; and those of freer principles, more indolent and languid. I have met with few exceptions in the compass of my acquaintance. I do deliberately think that the more persons enter into the pecul- iarities of the gospel, and the more regard they pay to the sacrifice of Christ and the influences of the Spirit, the more their own piety will increase, and the more zealous they will be to do good to the souls of others." *Ibid. vol. 1, p. 90.*

17*

Let them drink deep into the spirit and sentiments of the gospel, and give to all their discourses a *thoroughly Biblical character*—deriving their doctrines directly from the pure fountain of truth, and sustaining all their instructions by proofs from holy writ. This, at the present time, is supremely important. For, as was remarked in the last lecture, the great question at issue, between the friends and the enemies of evangelical religion in our country, is fast verging to a single point, and that is, whether the Bible is authority in matters of faith. This question settled, and the controversy is at an end. Here then, let the ministers of Christ take their stand; and committing themselves to the truth and authority of God's word, they need not fear the issue. Let them give themselves wholly to their work—their time, their talents, their studies, their all. While they gather around them the children and youth of their charge in the Sabbath school and Bible class—while they maintain stated meetings for conference and prayer, and visit from house to house, that they may learn the character and wants of their people, and thus know how to give to each a portion in due season, *let them look well to the pulpit*, and remember that *there* they are especially to lay out their strength and exhaust their energies, so that fervor, intelligence and life breathing through their ministrations and animating their prayers and sermons, the sanctuary may become a centre of attraction and interest to the surrounding population; and its services the means of their conversion and salvation. Every day and on all occasions, let them keep in view the great end of their ministry, and the solemn account which they must soon render of their stewardship unto Him who called them into his service and appointed them to watch for souls. Thus preaching and thus living, the interests which they are called to watch over and sustain will be secure. The Lord himself will lift up a standard against the enemy, and spread the pavilion of his love over the churches planted by our pilgrim fathers, and they shall stand and flourish, the glory and defence of our land, till the end of time.

2. Let us in the second place, inquire what means are to be used by *the members of our churches* in order to perpetuate their existence and promote their prosperity. In their *associated capacity* then, the first thing required of them, is, that they use *great caution* in the admission of members to their communion. It is plain from the Bible that our Lord Jesus Christ designed that the church, *his spiritual body*, should be composed only of living, spiritual members. This principle was uniformly regarded

and acted upon in the primitive churches; and also in the first churches of New-England. And while it was maintained, those churches flourished, and sent forth a healthful, regenerating influence over the land. But as the relinquishment of that principle brought on the papal apostacy, and shrouded the world in ages of darkness, so in New-England, it brought on the apostacy from the faith of our fathers, and has reduced many of the churches planted by their care, to mere societies of unsanctified, worldly men. And such must always be the consequence of opening the door of the church to persons who afford no evidence of piety. The necessary effect is to destroy the distinctive character of the church, as a holy community, and to introduce into it the seeds of corruption and decay.

Let the churches, then, that still retain the faith once delivered to the saints, carefully guard against the admission of persons to their communion, who furnish no satisfactory, scriptural evidence of having been born of God. It is only such as have been renewed by the Holy Spirit, that Christ judges worthy of a place in his spiritual temple; and if any of a different character are introduced into it, they will, in the day of trial, prove to be 'hay, wood, and stubble,' and only serve to weaken, deform and destroy the glorious edifice.

It is not enough considered, that the *strength* of a church is in the *piety* of its members—that its influence, in promoting the cause of God and the salvation of men, depends entirely upon its possessing a *holy, distinctive character*;—such a character as shall attract the attention of the world, and cause them to mark and consider its members, as a society of holy and devoted men and women. A church, possessing such a character, whether it be rich or poor, consist of few or many members, is 'a city set on a hill, that cannot be hid,'—a glorious light, lifted up on high, towards which the eyes of all will be directed, and whose influence, like the hand of God, will be felt turning back the tide of corruption, and elevating towards heaven and holiness a depraved and thoughtless generation. But, take away this holy, distinctive character from a church, and its renovating, life-giving influence is gone ; and itself, merged in the surrounding mass of worldliness and sin, no longer exists a glorious light to mark the way to heaven ; but a baleful meteor to mislead, bewilder and destroy.

In this view, it is seen to be a duty of immense importance, not only that the churches should guard against the *admission* of unworthy members to their fellowship, but also that they should maintain a careful inspection over their members, *when admitted,* and promptly exclude from their communion such as walk disorderly, or bring reproach upon the christian cause. There is, I fear, in many of our churches, a growing laxness in this respect. There is not that promptitude and decision in maintaining the discipline of the gospel, which existed in the better days of New-England. There is not in the members of our churches, that tenderness and carefulness in watching over and admonishing one another that there once was. In many cases, things are tolerated, which are a scandal to religion ; and persons are allowed to retain their standing in the church, whose lives are a reproach to their profession. These things, wherever they exist, are melancholy evidences of a low state of religion ; and no church in which they are tolerated, can reasonably expect to prosper. Its light will become dim—its energies be weakened, and the Holy Spirit, grieved by the unnatural intermixture of the pious and profane, will depart from its members, leaving them to declension, to division and ruin.

But we must here consider, more particularly, the the duties that are required of the members of our churches in their *individual capacity*. The circumstances, my brethren, in which the providence of God has placed you, impose upon you great and peculiar obligations. You are called to bear a part in sustaining the most precious interests that were ever entrusted to the hands of men. And that the sacred trust be not betrayed by you, it is first of all necessary, that you *look well to your personal religion.* If the spirit of piety be cold and languid in your bosoms, you can do nothing to any good purpose, in building up the cause of Christ. The church of which you are members will derive no benefit from your example, or your prayers; and in the community where you live, you will exert no influence in favor of vital godliness and the salvation of your fellow-men. *If the salt has lost its savor, it is good for nothing.* What the *times* demand, is a piety of the primitive stamp,—the deep-toned, self-denying, self-devoting piety, which characterized the fathers of New-England. Times of trial are at hand. The minds of men are powerfully excited; the public opinion is in a feverish state; there is extensively manifested an extreme restiffness under the restraints of religion; a strong disposition to break the bands and cast away the cords of allegiance to God; multitudes in all classes of society are setting themselves

against the Lord, and against his anointed ; infidelity and heresy, in a thousand forms, are spreading
through the land ; and the signs are not dubious, that
a crisis is approaching in the religious affairs of our
country, which will severely try the hearts of men,
and cause all to show whether they are for or against
the kingdom of Christ.

Let christians, then, look well to the foundation
on which they stand.   Let them see to it, that they
be thoroughly rooted and grounded in the truth,
eminently circumspect and holy in life, striving in all
things to exhibit the spirit of the gospel, and thus put
to silence the vain scoffs of ignorant objectors.   Let
them *fearlessly* assert their attachment to Christ,
and their belief of the distinguishing doctrines of his
gospel ; and let them consider, as devolved on *them,*
the sacred duty of sustaining, in their vigor and
purity, the institutions of our fathers, and of elevating
the standard of piety in the community where they
reside:

It is especially important at the present day, when
the enemies of religion, and errorists of every name
are combining to overthrow the faith once delivered
to the saints, that christians should carefully study
the evidences of that faith, in the only pure source
of evidence, the Bible ; and be ready always to give

to every one that asketh them, a reason of the hope that is in them. At a time like this, a superficial, traditionary faith will not suffice. Those who have no better foundation to stand upon, will show themselves unstable as water, carried about by every wind of doctrine.

Take, then, my friends, the great principle of the Reformation, and steadily act upon it, that the Bible, the Bible alone, is the rule of religion ; and while you embrace, in an intelligent affectionate faith, whatever doctrines are taught in the Bible, always be bold and decided in defending them against the cavils and reproaches of foolish and wicked men. *He* is unworthy of the christian name, who shrinks from an open avowal of the truth of God, or is afraid to defend what God has taught in his word.

'Cultivate a spirit of universal good will, and of amicable fellowship towards all those, of whatever sect or denomination, who differing from you in nonessentials, agree with you in the fundamentals of religion.' If others assert exclusive rights, or set up exclusive terms of communion, *unchurching* all who do not exactly agree with them in outward forms and ceremonies, imitate them not. All such exclusive claims are wrong in themselves, and cannot fail, in the end, to injure the denomination that asserts them.

18

Ever act on the truly liberal and catholic principle of receiving and treating all as christians whom you have evidence to believe that Christ has received. Never cherish towards any such, of whatever name or sect they may be, any other than a spirit of christian kindness and love. Never encroach upon their rights ; never attempt, by unfair means, to proselyte an individual from their connexion ; never throw the slightest obstacle in the way of their prosperity.

I mean not by this to encourage indifference to error, or the slightest deriliction of your own distinctive principles. On the contrary, I would have you regard all error as hurtful ; and for the principles of your own order, I would ever have you cherish, and on all proper occasions, express, a strong and decided preference. But I would also have you show, that you make a distinction between great things and little—between essentials and non-essentials in religion ; and that, while you love and prefer your own denomination, you can, at the same time, extend the hand of fellowship to all who love the Lord Jesus Christ in sincerity and truth.

In all attempts to build up the cause of Christ, scrupulously avoid a worldly, selfish policy. The religion of Christ frowns on such a policy ; and demands to be promoted only by plain, open, honest conduct, proceeding from motives that will bear to be inspected in the face of day.

Carefully guard also against connecting, in any manner, the interests of the church with the affairs of state, or the politics of the day. *Let there be no political combinations for religious purposes, nor religious combinations for political purposes.* Experience proves that the tendency of all such combinations is to corrupt religion and destroy the energies of the church. *My kingdom*, says our Lord, *is not of this world.—Not of this world in its spirit ; not of this world in its aims ; not of this world in the means of advancing its prosperity, and extending its influence on earth.* Every day, I am more and more convinced, that the great point to be aimed at in this country is to withdraw the church, as far as possible, from the collisions of politics, and the strife of party spirit. In these angry times, religion has nothing to hope from civil government ; I wish I could add, it has nothing to fear from it. The only true and safe policy is to let the church stand on its own immutable foundation—the truth and promise of God ; and to adopt only such means in building it up as are sanctioned in his word. Not that christians are to take *no part* in the political concerns of their country. They are freemen ;—they possess the rights and lie under the responsibilities of freemen, and can by no means be excused from bearing a part in sustaining the interests and promoting the welfare of the community of which they are members.   Especially does the right of suffrage impose on them a very sacred duty ; and in the exercise of that right, they are solemnly bound to commit themselves to the dictation of no party, but with an enlightened conscience, and in the fear of God, always to withhold their support from *bad men* of every name, and to give their votes in favor of such as are best qualified for the duties of office, to whatever denomination or party they belong.   I will just add in this connection, that so *totally depraved* are the politics of the day, that I see not how a christian can enter fully into the spirit of them, or commit himself to any party, to go all lengths with them, without doing violence to his conscience, and greatly injuring his christian character and influence.   Certain I am, that if the churches of our country are to prosper, or if the members in communion with them are to grow in faith, and love, and usefulness, they must be preserved from the *mania* of party zeal, and stand aloof from the conflicts of ambition, and the din of political controversy.   Their sphere of influence is more retired and silent.   It is in the sanctuary, in the family, in the every-day intercourse of life, in diffusing around them the spirit of holiness, and exemplifying in conduct the pure and blessed principles of the gospel.

Here, my brethren, is the appropriate sphere of christian enterprize and action ;—these the means by which the churches of New-England are to be strengthened and their influence extended through the land. Let a higher standard of piety be set up in these churches, and all the members of them aim in their temper and life, to make a complete exhibition of the spirit of the gospel. Let family religion be revived and maintained in all their households, and the blessing of God be daily and piously sought to descend upon them and their children. No duty is more reasonable than this—none more conscientiously performed by our ancestors, and none contributed more to that purity of morals and elevation of piety which distinguished the better days of New-England. Indeed nothing is plainer than that if there is no religion in the family, there is none in the church, and none in the community ; and all hope of piety in the rising generation is vain.

Let the Sabbath of the Lord be honored as at the beginning ; and every professor of religion make it a matter of conscience to observe that holy day, according to the design of its appointment. This is a duty

18*

of prime importance.   At a time when the Lord's day is every where profaned with impunity by wicked men, it becomes christians to keep the day with peculiar strictness—to throw the whole weight of their example in favor of its due observance; and thus to stay, at least for a while, the sweeping ruin which the general desecration of the Sabbath threatens to bring upon the country.

Look well to the education of your children.   Let the school, the academy, the college; their associates, amusements, and occupations in life, all be chosen with reference to their spiritual and immortal well-being.   Having dedicated them to God in baptism, and thus solemnly engaged to bring them up for him, see to it that you always remember your vows, and never act inconsistently with them.   So live yourselves, and so train up your children, that you may point them to your example and say, Tread in my steps and go with me to heaven.   This duty, always important, is supremely so at the present day.

When Jesuits were sent among the Waldenses to entice them from the truth to idolatry, they returned amazed, professing that children of seven years old knew more of the scriptures, and of the mysteries of the gospel, than many of their doctors did.   This suggests your duty, and points out the means, by which you may hope to save your children, and qualify them to receive the precious inheritance which must soon pass from your hands to theirs. The errors, the temptations, and sins which every where surround the young, can be averted only by bringing them early under the influence of christian instruction and christian principle.

Be it then your great concern to train up your children for God and glory,—to imbue their young and tender minds with the principles of the gospel and with the love of virtue and goodness.

Let christian mothers, especially engage with zeal in this divine work. With the first dawnings of affection and intelligence in your little ones, let your doctrine drop as the rain and distill as the dew. Early attach them to the institutions and principles of the pilgrims. Tell them the story of their toils and sufferings; make them acquainted with the excellence of their character, with the grandeur of their enterprize, and the rich blessings that have flowed from their counsels and their efforts ; and while with pious care you labor to train them up in the nurture and admonition of the Lord, pour over them the incessant fervent prayer, that the God of the pilgrims will be their God, and their portion forever.

Let your hearts be much set on revivals of reli-

gion.   Never forget that the churches of New England were planted in the spirit of revivals ; that they
have hitherto existed and prospered by revivals, and
that if they are to exist and prosper in time to come,
it must be by the same cause which has from the
first been their glory and defence.

Let the irreligious and the profane, let infidels and
scoffers discard the influences of the Holy Spirit, and
denounce revivals of religion as fanaticism and delusion ; but let christians, let the descendants of the pilgrims, never be ashamed to own their dependance
on the Holy Spirit, or to confess that it is not by
might nor by power, but by the spirit of the Lord
that his kingdom is to be built up in this fallen world.

Finally, ever bear it in mind, that you 'have but a
little while to live, and that your great business here
is to prepare yourselves, your children and your fellow men for the scenes of eternal judgment.   Live
then as becometh those who must so soon go hence
and give up their account unto God.   Live not for
time, but for eternity ; not for yourselves, but for him
who died for you and rose again.   Then shall you
see the cause of God prospering around you ; the
heritage of your fathers descending in undiminished
glory to bless your posterity, and yourselves cheered
in the decline of life by these happy visions, shall die

in peace and rise to become pillars in the temple of God to go no more out forever.

3. Permit me now to address a few words to the members of congregations, considered as distinct from the churches. The religious institutions of our fathers, my friends, have strong claims on your steady attachment, and vigorous support. They have been bequeathed to you by men eminent for their talents, their learning and piety. For two hundred years they have been diffusing through this community, the blessings of knowledge, of virtue and religion. Under their enlightening and sanctifying influence, many of your ancestors have been gathered into the fold of Christ and prepared for his kingdom of glory. Through the unwearied care of a long succession of pious men, and the watchful providence of a gracious God, they have come down to you, retaining, still, much of their original simplicity and excellence ; and now the blessed inheritance is placed in your hands to be transmitted to those who are to come after you. What remains then but that you cherish an enlightened, uniform attachment to these institutions, and support them by your combined influence. There are indeed the best and most solid reasons for such attachment. You have seen their accordance with the order of the primitive churches,—

their adaptation to the genius of our civil institutions, and to all the great purposes of religious worship. You have also been called to survey, though imperfectly indeed, the happy consequences which have resulted from them, both to this community and the country at large. Never then forsake these institutions. Never be backward to bear your full proportion of the expense necessary to support them. That parent, or master of a family, who retires from the house of God, or withdraws his name as a member of an ecclesiastical society, because he is unwilling to pay a little tax for the support of the gospel, *wrongs his own soul and inflicts the deepest injury on the welfare of his family and society.* For a little paltry lucre, he does that which will probably prove the ruin of himself, and be the means of entailing sin and ruin upon his posterity. Ever then avoid such a course of conduct as you would avoid the road to death. It is mean, it is sinful, it is destructive to your best interests both in this world and in that which is to come.* You owe it to the

* The author states this with a melancholy array of facts before him. Individuals, and families, and, in some cases, whole neighborhoods, once exemplary for their morals and general respect for religion and religious institutions, has he known to be reduced to a state little short of heathenism, by an act of covetousness or passion, in breaking away from their connection with ec-

memory of your pilgrim ancestors, you owe it as a debt of gratitude to those who have lived here before you, and from whom you have received this goodly heritage ; you owe it to your children and to posterity that are fast rising up to fill your places in society, to throw the shield of your entire influence around the institutions of our venerated fathers, and to defend them against all assaults of enemies.

Do not understand me to inculcate a *bigoted* attachment to your own order,—an attachment which shall lead you to set up exclusive pretensions, and to look down with a haughty eye upon all other denominations. This would be an error as directly opposed to the true principles of Congregationalism, as it is to the spirit of the gospel. But while you cherish sentiments of true liberality towards other

clesiastical society. A man is covetous, and unwilling to give any thing for the support of the gospel ; or he takes offence at something said or done by the minister, or at the misconduct of some member of the church, or at some supposed mismanagement or improper act on the part of the congregation,—forthwith, he throws in his certificate—withdraws himself and his family from the house of God and from all connection with the stated means of grace. This is a case of very frequent occurrence ; and it is, much as if a man, to gratify his avarice, or revenge some injury done him by his neighbor, should fire his own house, or sign a warrant for the exclusion of himself and his posterity from the kingdom of God.

denominations that differ from you in forms of worship and modes of external order, never be indifferent to the superior claims of *your own ;* always be ready to assert a preference for *your own*, and by all proper means, strive to promote its prosperity and extend its influence.

Be not moved, if at any time you hear it asserted, that the ecclesiastical order to which you belong, is *schismatical ;* that the ministry under which you sit, is unauthorized ; that the churches belonging to your denomination, are no churches ; and that the ordinances administered in them, are invalid and nugatory. Such charges and denunciations should rather excite your pity than alarm your fears ; and should be listened to with the same unconcern that you feel, when a " partizan of the Papacy denounces you for rejecting the supremacy of the Pope, and questions the possibility of your salvation out of the church of Rome."

Remember the interesting relation you sustain to past and future generations, and be faithful to the sacred trust committed to you. Above all, remember that the best and most perfect forms of worship, are after all, *but forms ;* and if unanimated by the spirit of true religion, are only as sounding brass and tinkling cymbals. Never forget that religion is a personal thing ; that it has its seat in the heart, and is indispensable to your standing approved of God in the great day of account. Enter, then, without delay, into the spirit of the institutions which you inherit from your fathers ; be christians in deed and in truth, and thus be prepared to join your pious ancestors in that blessed world where distinctions of name and sect are unknown ; where all who love the Lord Jesus in sincerity, are embraced in one vast, united and happy assembly ; where their worship and communion are perfect and everlasting.

4. I turn, in conclusion, to the young, especially to young men, the rising hope of the church and of society. Ardently attached as I am to the principles and order of the Congregational churches, and to the institutions of my country, I look round with deep emotion, upon those into whose hands the precious inheritance is soon to pass. I behold the aged fathers and mothers, who have long borne the heat and burden of the day, passing from the stage of life and dropping, one after another, into the unseen world. I see others of my own age, the acting members of society, fast treading after the aged, and soon to be gathered with them to the great congregation of the dead. The young are rising up to fill our places, destined to act a little moment amidst those

transcient scenes, then to disappear, giving place in their turn to another generation. O how affecting these changes! How soon to be experienced! God, my young friends, has placed you in circumstances of deep and solemn interest. You are called to cherish the memory of your ancestors, to bind their principles to your hearts, to defend and maintain their institutions, and transmit them unimpaired, to those who shall come after you. Those ancestors, my friends, are worthy of your veneration and love; their principles worthy of your deepest affection and esteem; their institutions worthy of your warmest attachment and most decided support.

They have, indeed, often been vilified and reproached; they will be vilified and reproached again; but this alters not their merits, nor renders them the less deserving of your esteem and support. The cry of bigotry and superstition and persecution will be echoed again and again. You will hear it repeated a thousand times that Calvin burnt Servetus, that the Puritans persecuted the Quakers and Baptists, and were the abettors of a gloomy and intolerant religion. This stale and silly slang is in the mouth of every enemy of religion, who has only wit enough to repeat what others have said before him; and has, time out of mind, furnished the standing topics of ridicule and reproach to all who hate the spirit and institutions of the Pilgrims. A sufficient reply is—Look at results. Men do not gather grapes of thorns, nor figs of thistles. The works of the Pilgrims speak for themselves. They furnish their own defence. But who are they that are so fond of raising the cry of bigotry and superstition? Are they the truly candid, the truly pious, the truly liberal? The very last characteristics to which such persons are entitled. They cry bigotry against others, but are themselves the greatest bigots; and are tolerant towards none but the enemies of evangelical truth and serious religion.

Be not moved then, my young friends, at the charge of bigotry, while you stand up in defence of essential principles, and show yourselves decided in supporting the institutions of your ancestors. The charge falls on others rather than yourselves; and furnishes an occasion of glorying rather than of shame.

But Calvin burnt Servetus, Calvin burnt Servetus—yes, Calvin burnt Servetus. He did not. He neither burnt him, nor instigated his burning. He endeavored to plead him off from the sentence pronounced upon him by the Senate of Geneva, and to obtain for him a commutation of his punishment for something less severe. But what if he did procure the death of Servetus? Does this prove the Bible untrue, or the system of doctrine usually denominated Calvinistic, false? or that the Orthodox of New-England hold that system just as Calvin taught it? or that they are advocates for the persecution and burning of heretics? Nothing of all this. Why then are these things said? *To bring reproach upon the truth, and to excite odium against the friends of evangelical religion.* But was Calvin, or the Purtians the only persecutors that ever lived? Did not Socinus, the founder of Socinianism, persecute Francis Davides, superintendent of the Socinian churches in Transylvania? Did he not procure his being thrown into prison, where, after languishing six years, he died?* Are not christian men and christian women at the present day, in various Cantons of Switzerland, persecuted, imprisoned, and banished from the country, for holding the evangelical doctrines, by those who style themselves liberal christians?† I am ashamed to state these things, and would not, but for the sake of rescuing the truth from perversion, and defending it against the re-

* See Waterman's Life of Calvin, p. 126, and Hist. of Diss. vol. IV. p. 244.

† Chris. Spectator, 1830, p. 99—326.

proaches that have been cast upon it.*   Let the
doctrines and institutions of the fathers of New-England stand or fall on their own merits ; but let no

* The allusion in this sentence, and the reason for introducing
the preceding paragraphs, will be understood by those who were
present at the delivery of the lecture.   To others it is a matter of
too little importance to need explanation.

Many, whose standing argument against the doctrines of the
Orthodox is, that Calvin burnt Servetus, seem not to recollect
the persecutions which in this nineteenth century the Unitarians
have carried on, and are still carrying on, against the friends of
evangelical religion in Switzerland.   They are wont also to pass
over silently the act of persecution perpetrated by Socinus against
Davides, while at the same time they keep up a constant deafen-
ing outcry against the murderous Calvin for his conduct towards
Servetus.   The following facts may help to a better understanding of this subject.   They are from Bogue and Bennett's Hist. of
Diss. vol. IV. p. 244 : " If it be alleged that Socinus left Davides
to the civil power, the same excuse may be made for Calvin. When
it is asserted that this reformer ruled in Geneva, so that the acts
of the government were his own, it may be replied that the government once banished Calvin himself, who declared before Servetus came to Geneva, that it would not be in his power to save
him ; so that his influence was little more than that of the Socinians in Transylvania, who had acquired such an ascendant thát the
man whom they persecuted was sent to die in a jail.   Calvin labored to dissuade a stranger, who was viewed with horror, from
coming to a place where the laws, which had been enacted long
before by the emperor, would consign him to the flames ;* but the
Socinians saw their brother, the superintendent of their churches,
hurled from his honors to a dungeon ; and what efforts did they
make to save him ?   The death of Servetus, which was cruel indeed, was inflicted for what all the reformers, as well as Calvin,
deemed damnable heresies, worthy of death, the blasphemy of de-

* See Mosheim for the above facts.
19*

dishonest, illiberal measures be adopted to bring them into disrepute, or to arm ignorance or prejudice against them.   Those doctrines and institutions, my young friends, will bear examination.   Examine them ; examine them for yourselves ; examine them in the light of God's word ; examine them in the light which the experience of two centuries has cast upon them ; examine them in the light which beams from the virtue, the intelligence, the piety, the happiness that so signally bless this fair portion of our land ; and sure I am, that the effect will be a deepened conviction of their excellence, and of the duty of maintaining them.

Come forward then, ye who are so soon to be the acting members of society, and possess the goodly inheritance that has come down to you from your

grading the Son of God to an ordinary man, his death to mere martyrdom, and his worship to idolatry.   But the Socinians who are supposed to outstrip all others in liberal principles, hunted Davides to prison from political motives, lest the odium under which they labored should be augmented.   Socinus *publicly* stigmatized the adherents of Davides as semi-Jews, and urged the unfortunate man to renounce his error ; but *privately* he acknowledged (as in all reason and consistency he was compelled to do) that it was a mere nothing—nay, no error at all, but a proof of strong faith ; so that Davides was made a sacrifice, not to honest bigotry, but to mere finesse.   The aggravated guilt of Socinus is, indeed, no excuse for that of Calvin ; but it may suffice to expose the conduct of his followers, who adduce the crime of the latter, as a proof of the blackness of his character and of the intolerant tendency of his doctrines."

fathers. Never forsake that inheritance; never think lightly of it; never withhold from it the aid of your counsels, your efforts, your prayers. Wherever your lot in life may be cast, glory in your ancestry; show yourselves the worthy descendants of the Pilgrims; and do all in your power to revive, extend, and perpetuate their spirit, their principles and their institutions. Be not beguiled by any of those false-hearted, delusive systems, which, while they are forever chanting forth the praises of their own liberality, are distinguished for nothing so much as for their *illiberality* towards all who hold the distinguishing doctrines of the Bible, and are firm and decided in support of them. Bring all such systems to the test. Be not deceived by fair speeches and kind professions. Words may be softer than oil, and yet be drawn swords. Inquire whether the advocates of such systems are men of piety, are men of prayer, are men of devotedness to God and the good of mankind; whether the systems themselves are accordant with the truth of God, adapted to your wants as sinners, fitted to cheer and comfort you in the dying hour, and to prepare you for the great day of judgment and account. If they endure not this test, forbear to embrace them, and abide still in the old paths, the good way, and you shall find rest for your souls.

Cast an eye forward to the scenes before you. Recollect that you are born for immortality ; that you have begun an existence which is never to end, and that your condition, eternal ages after the heavens and the earth shall have passed away, depends on the character you form in this state of your probation. Rise up then to the great work of preparation for immortal honor and blessedness. Remember from whom you are descended ; into whose labors you have entered ; what privileges you enjoy and to what heights in glory you may rise, if you forfeit not the bright inheritance by forsaking the God of your fathers and going after other gods.

It is recorded of the ancient Scythians, that when in battle they were overpowered by their enemies, they would retreat till they came to the graves of their fathers, and there take their stand nor yield but in death.

And now, could I make my voice resound through New-England, I would assemble the youth, *the young men* of the land around the graves of their fathers, and there I would swear them to be true to their memories and to maintain their principles and institutions with their latest breath. If you fail here, my friends ; if you forsake the God of your fathers and alienate the precious inheritance which they have bequeathed to you, O how will you offend against the venerable exiles, who came here and toiled and suffered and died, that they might leave their example and their labors a blessing to their descendants and the world ! How will you offend against the dearest privileges and hopes of this community, and draw down upon your memories the reproaches of posterity for having robbed them of their birthright ? The sacred shades of the Pilgrims will testify against you ; the graves of Hooker and Stone and Haynes, of Robinson and Winthrop and Cotton will testify against you ; God himself will testify against you, and provoked by an ungrateful dereliction of truth and duty on the part of those whom he has distinguished above all others by the abundance of his blessings, he will inscribe on the temples of New-England, *the glory is departed.*

But I read brighter auspices in the destiny of New-England. The God, who remembers mercy unto a thousand generations, will not forget the children of the Pilgrims ; nor the churches planted and nurtured by their prayers and tears. He will still watch over them for good ; will still defend and bless them with his continual presence and favor ; and when their present pastors and members shall be gathered to their final home, other ministers and christians will be raised up to occupy these pulpits and fill these churches; and thus the divine light kindled by the Pilgrims amidst icy storms and dreary wilds, will continue to expand and brighten, from generation to generation, till it mingles and is lost in the glories of millennial day.

Check Out More Titles From HardPress Classics Series In this collection we are offering thousands of classic and hard to find books. This series spans a vast array of subjects — so you are bound to find something of interest to enjoy reading and learning about.

Subjects:
Architecture
Art
Biography & Autobiography
Body, Mind &Spirit
Children & Young Adult
Dramas
Education
Fiction
History
Language Arts & Disciplines
Law
Literary Collections
Music
Poetry
Psychology
Science
…and many more.

Visit us at www.hardpress.net

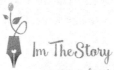